Run From There
A Biography of Edward P. Hurt

Run From There
A Biography of Edward P. Hurt

Herman L. Wade

A Biography of a Great Black Coach whose vision continues to impact the lives of thousands

Copyright © 2003 by Herman L. Wade

(Photographs courtesy of Morgan State University Archives and also the Edward P. Hurt Collection)

All rights reserved. No part of this book may be used or reproduced in any manner whatsoever without written permission of the author.

Printed in the United States of America.

ISBN: 1-932205-78-0

Word Association Publishers
205 5th Avenue,
Tarentum, PA 15084
www.wordassociation.com

Dedication

With special thanks to William "Bill" Brown, Roy Cragway, Samuel LaBeach, Dr. Jo-an Rodenhauser, PhD. of Morgan State University, Edith Murungi of Soper Library MSU, Rev. Tanya S. Wade, and Betty Wade for their assistance in the compiling of this tribute to Coach.

Also..

To the Morgan Bears who were tested on the battlefield of athletic endeavor and have maintained that fighting "Bears" spirit throughout life, and to Edward P. Hurt (Coach), who gave us a creed for life: *"Run From There."*

And...

The "Flying Four"

Otis Johnson, James Rogers, Josh Culbreath, and Herman Wade

For my daughter, Rhonda Joy

1967-2001

A poem Eddie P. Hurt loved and lived by:

I'm tired of sailing my little ship
close to the harbor bar
I want to launch out in the deep
Out there where the big ones are
And if my frail craft should fail
To sail the deep sea o'er
Then I'd rather go down in the deep
Than to be lulled to sleep
By the sheltered shore.

Author Unknown

Whenever things were tough, Coach Edward P. Hurt would map out the half-time strategy and then call on his good friend and colleague Talmadge "Marse" Hill, who would, with the eloquence of a fire-and-brimstone Baptist preacher, fire his boys up – closing with the poem above.

The proceeds of this book, less publishing costs, will be donated to the Morgan State University scholarship fund in the name of Coach and Mrs. Edward P. Hurt.

COACH • MENTOR • TEACHER • LEADER

United States Olympic Coach
United States Olympic Committee

Coach of the year, Washington Pig Skin Club 1949

One of the outstanding football coaches of all time.
University of Texas 1950

U.S. Olympic Coach

Track Coach of the year
Track & Field News 1950

President IC4A Track
Leaders 1968-1970

Coach USA/USSR
Kiev Russia 1965

Who's Who in
Black America

Pan America Games
Coach 1959

NCAA Track Coach
of the year 1970

Hall of Fame
Track & Field 1975

Ref. Penn Relays

Edward P. Hurt

Omega Psi Phi Fraternity
Ambassador of Good Will to
America on Behalf of his Race

Biographical Sketch of Edward Paulette Hurt

Edward Paulette Hurt, Professor of Health and Physical Education, Director of Athletics and Coach of Track and Field, Morgan State College, Baltimore, Maryland.

Retired in 1970

PERSONAL DATA:	Born February 12, 1900, Brookneal, VA; married to the former Beatrice Reid of East Orange, NJ; no children. Died March 24, 1989.
EDUCATION:	Elementary Education in Brookneal, VA; high school education in Lynchburg, VA; A.B. degree in Mathematics, Howard University, Washington, D.C.; M.S. degree in Health and Physical Education, Columbia University; LL.D. degree, Morgan State College, 1970
TEACHING:	Teacher of Mathematics and Assistant Coach, Virginia Seminary and College, Lynchburg, VA, 1921; Head Coach, 1925-1929.
	Faculty of Morgan State College from 1929-1970, where he served as Instructor of Mathematics, Coach of Basketball (1929-1947), Acting Head of Physical Education Department, Head Coach of

HIGHLIGHTS OF COACHING CAREER:

Football (1929-1959), Coach of Track and Field, and Director of Athletics. Retired in 1970.

Football: Hurt-coached Elevens (1930-1959) won 14 Central Intercollegiate Athletic Association (CIAA) championships; 1932-1939, teams played 54 games without a defeat, one of the longest unbroken strings on record.

Basketball: Hurt-coached Cagers won 4 CIAA championships, 3 of them won in 3 consecutive years, 1931, 1932, and 1933.

Track and Field: Hurt coached Morgan teams; produced 8 individual National Collegiate Athletic Association (NCAA) champions; 12 National AAU champions in individual events; 3 National Collegiate Athletic Relay championships; 1 Olympian Champion (George Rhoden, record holder in the 400-meter dash), and 1 Olympian 3rd-place winner (Josh Culbreath, 400-meter hurdles); 11 individual and 8 relay championships at the Penn Relays.

Morgan has won 18 track and field championships in the CIAA since entering the Conference in 1930.

HONORS: All-American End, Lincoln University, 1918; Howard University, 1919 and 1920.

Coach of the Year by Washington Pigskin Club, 1949.

One of the Outstanding Football Coaches of All Times, University of Texas, 1950.

Track Coach of the year, *Track and Field News*, 1950

Morgan State College Student Council Scroll for Unusual Achievement, 1950.

Edward P. Hurt Gymnasium at Morgan State College, named in his honor, dedicated in 1952.

Baltimore Urban League's Distinguished Service Award (in the field of athletics), 1953.

Elected to the Helms foundation Hall of Fame (track coaches), 1953.

Morgan State College Alumni Award, 25 years, 1954.

Howard University Department of Physical Education Achievement Award, 1958.

Morgan State College Varsity "M" Club Award, 1959.

Omega Psi Phi Fraternity Plaque (Builder of Character and Champions), 1959.

Listed among football coaches of the year, 1959. Only black selected by member of Coaches Association of America and Associated Press.

Coaching Staff, Pan-American Games, 1959.

U.S. Olympic Track and Field Games Committee, 1960-1972.

Referee — Penn Relays, 1961

United States Olympic Committee Award for Service to the Olympics, 1964.

Coaching Staff, USA Men's Track and Field Team, Tokyo, Japan, Olympics, 1964.

YMCA (Harlem Branch) Sports Award, 1965.

Jerusalem Temple #4, Baltimore, MD – Merit of Sports Award, 1965.

Coaching Staff, USA/USSR Dual Track Meet in Kiev, Russia, 1965.

Howard University Alumni Achievement Award, 1966.

CIAA Collegiate, Civic and Professional Award, 1967.

President, IC4A Track Coaches Association, 1968-1970.

Maryland Physical Fitness Award, 1969.

NCAA Indoor Track Coach of the Year, 1970.

Governor's Award for 40 Years of Service to the State of Maryland, 1970.

Referee—NCAA Track and Field Championships (College Division), 1971.

Elected to the Helms Foundation Hall of Fame (Athletic Directors), 1972.

Elected to the Morgan State Athletic Hall of Fame, 1974.

Elected to the National Track and Field Hall of Fame of the United States of America, 1975.

Prince Hall Masonry Bicentennial Award, 1975.

Who's Who in the East, 1977-78, 1981-82.

Afro American Newspaper Honor Roll.

Afro American Newspaper Coach of the Year.

Henry Arthur Keane Trophy – Football.

Who's Who in Black America.

Black Colleges Coaches Hall of Fame.

Mayor's Award. Baltimore, CT

National Association of Intercollegiate Athletics Hall of Fame.

MEMBERSHIPS: Mayor's committee on Education and Aging. Omega Psi Phi Fraternity, USA Track Coaches Association, and NAACP.

INTRODUCTION

History is resplendent with the names of great people who, through courage, strong character, and intellectual perseverance, have climbed the mountaintop. People who, through great trials and often hard and cruel circumstances, have not looked upon their particular situation but have ignored the facts with an abiding, fervent faith and hope and have transcended the levels of their peers and risen to the top. Who can say: do the times make the man, or does the man make the times?

What more befitting a scenario than to find oneself in the period of history in which people have been oppressed, deprived both materially and spiritually; people who have suffered economic deprivation and spiritual dehumanization, and have been left out of the main stream of public and national affairs, but being of sturdy stock and possessed of a gift for survival, were slowly coming to life and seeking their God-given rights as human beings and their constitutional rights as Americans?

The year was 1900, not a particularly good year for black men, just 35 years after the Emancipation Proclamation. On the 12th of February of that year, a child was born to Isaac and Sarah Hurt.

Halley's comet was not flashing across the heavens that year, nor was there any other ominous celestial display to mark that year in remembrance of Eddie's birthday. No black man prior to Martin Luther King in 1985 had achieved the necessary acclaim or notoriety for his peers to honor his birthday. The future in 1900 for the black man was not bright. However, neither the bleakness of the hour nor the abysmal projection for the future could dim the hope of Isaac and Sarah Hurt on that day in 1900. When a child is born there is always hope–hope for a happy life and hope for achievement. Not even the darkest moment can dim the hopes of loving parents. It was into such an atmosphere that Edward Paulette Hurt was born on that day in the small town of Brookneal, Virginia.

If his parents could have seen the future, they would have been elated because their son, "Eddie," was destined to lift a small black college to heights of greatness, break down social barriers, and become one of the first black college coaches to receive national acclaim as a coach and educator. Also he would turn great numbers of young black athletes loose on the world with the words and the spirit of his monogram "run from there" engraved on their consciousnesses. To those Bears trained under Eddie Hurt, "run from there" meant, "give it all you've got." It was indeed the type of message that motivated boys to become men and enabled them to face the vicissitudes of life that they, as black men in their era, were destined to face.

So it was that Eddie Hurt became an educator, mathematician, coach, and father figure for thousands of young men. He was an ambassador for his race, a tactician and strategist to play and coach with the best in the country.

The 19th Annual Meeting of the Colored Intercollegiate Athletic Association (CIAA) met at North Carolina State college, Durham, North Carolina, on December 13 and 14, 1929. If Eddie Hurt had been a superstitious man, Friday the 13th might have crushed his hopes. However, on that day he appeared before the CIAA committee, and in a clear, confident voice, requested that Morgan College be admitted to the conference. After some discussion, it was moved and seconded that Morgan College become a member of the CIAA beginning with the school year 1930-1931.

Although Eddie Hurt was not superstitious, he had plenty to worry about. His team had played many of the CIAA teams, and the results were discouraging. In 1929, the football team's record against four CIAA opponents was 0 wins, 4 losses – Morgan 7, Lincoln 19; Morgan 0, St. Paul 6; Morgan 0, Virginia State 13; Morgan 7, Virginia Union 19 (CIAA Bulletin). Eddie knew that the conference members were all certain they could fatten their records against the new college with a young, inexperienced coach.

The CIAA was organized in 1911 at Hampton University. The charter members were Hampton, Howard, Lincoln, Union, and Shaw Universities. At the time of Morgan's entrance into the conference, the CIAA consisted of the following black colleges: Howard University, Washington, D.C.; Lincoln University, Lincoln, Pennsylvania; Virginia State College, Petersburg, Virginia; Union University, Richmond, Virginia; North Carolina A&T College, Greensboro, North Carolina; Shaw University, Raleigh, North Carolina; Virginia Seminary, Lynchburg, Virginia; State College, Durham, North Carolina; Hampton Institute, Hampton, Virginia; J.C. Smith University, Charlotte, North Carolina; Livingston College, North Carolina.

The impact that the organization had on the development of colored sports and athletes can be seen from this excerpt from the 20th Annual Session in 1931:

> " This endeavor on the part of the association to develop wholesome, clean athletics has been supported and approved by both public and press, and this endorsement has been shown by the increased attendance at the games and greater public interest. The association is constantly widening the scope of its work. Last year three meets were approved in the hope of encouraging greater participation in track athletics."

It was into this type of organization that Eddie, with foresight and imagination, led Morgan College. At this time, some of the finest black men of this century were laying the foundation for a real thrust at the national pastime of this great country—its love of competitive sports. Eddie, not wanting to be a lame duck in such a powerful conference, immediately began to use the gifts with which he had been endowed.

He knew the game, but the responsibilities facing the 30-year-old athletic director were awesome. He had to develop the entire college sports program, intercollegiate and intramural. Faced with limited facilities, a small budget, and no assistant coaches, the task would have caused most men to call it a day, but not

Eddie Hurt. Using his imagination, organizational skills, and just plain ingenuity, he managed to teach not only trigonometry and calculus, but also to do the coaching as well.

In 1930, he shocked the entire Conference. Not only did the Bears win the CIAA football championship but also the basketball championship. His football record that first year was particularly spectacular.

It is fair to say that the CIAA Conference colleges began to recognize the talents of Eddie Hurt. What was it about this man that gave him such drive to win and to work so arduously? Perhaps it was the heart he displayed while playing basketball around Lynchburg, Virginia during the early years or later on as a Virginia Seminary athletic great.

Eddie demonstrated his desire and determination while playing offensive and defensive end for Lincoln University in 1918 where he was named All American. As the story goes, Eddie showed up for football practice at Lincoln one day, and the head coach was none other than the great Fritz Pollard of Yale and of Ivy League fame. He took one look at Eddie's small frame and almost dismissed him. On a hunch he said to Eddie, "I'm going to carry the ball and I want you to stop me, if you can." Until the day he died, Eddie always said that he still feels the shattering, bone-crushing impact as Pollard repeatedly sprinted around left end, and Eddie met him head on. Pollard never once made it past Eddie, and from that day on, Eddie was the starting end. Although he displayed great desire, talent, and determination that day, Eddie couldn't possibly imagine the situations that he would be called upon to tackle as his career led him into the pitfalls of the American social system – the separate but equal philosophy as defined by the Supreme Court (Plessy v. Ferguson, 1896, U.S. Supreme Court). This ruling caused some of the greatest black athletes of all times to miss completely the opportunity to participate as professionals on the same level as their fellow Americans.

Prior to Eddie's taking over Morgan's athletic program, Morgan had, in 1926-27, one of the best Negro athletes of all time as well as one of the world's finest scholars, as its athletic director: Charles Drew, of Amhurst University, 1926-1927. Years later, Drew received his doctorate and was hailed as a pioneer and developer of techniques in blood preservation in the 1940s, a discovery that saved countless WWII lives. He was named Director of the Red Cross Blood Bank.

The Morgan basketball team under Charles Drew was outstanding. They played the great New York Renaissance Basketball team and unexpectedly won the game. Many at the time considered the Renaissance team to be the best in the world.

The college scandals of the past 50 years concerning the conflict between winning and academic standards can help us appreciate the foresight of Eddie and the other men of the CIAA.

The goals of the CIAA were not just about winning, but about the development of the whole man. These goals helped to supplement Eddie's own philosophy concerning winning and education. In 1932, the president of the CIAA, James T. Taylor, wrote an article entitled "Major Accomplishments of the CIAA 1932." It appeared in the CIAA Bulletin 1932, 21st Annual Session:

> "There have been sharp curves, rough spots and bumps, but in spite of these difficult places in the road to success, all impartial critics must admit that the CIAA has kept its eyes on its final destination, wholesome competitive sports in Negro Colleges. The CIAA has a scholarship requirement for intercollegiate participation. The institutions have not always lived up to this requirement, but at the present time machinery is set up by the association that will make it difficult for any school to violate this agreement. It is a fact that the sentiment among facilities and students is preponderantly for the strict enforcement of this requirement."

That same year, James O. Spencer, president of Morgan State College, wrote this article, entitled "College Athletes." It also appeared in the proceedings of the 21st Annual Session:

> "The spirit of the contest should reflect the highest and truest ideals of the college as a whole.... It is to be feared that college football and basketball will become professionalized and go the way of baseball unless the profit motive can be controlled and limited. Schools need the money but should not sell their birthright of real clean sport for a mess of commercial pottage however savory."

In the late '20s, Eddie found one situation totally unacceptable. The NCAA (National Collegiate Athletic Association) was conducting track meets in Baltimore. Colored athletes were permitted to participate, but they ran their events on the second day of the meet. They were running against the clock, and as any good athlete knows, this is extremely difficult. Most individuals who understand sports are aware of the great track victories of Jesse Owens in the 1936 Olympics. Jesse's story of success and victories is equaled only by the obstacles and prejudices he had to overcome to achieve his greatness. Eddie Hurt also found the problem of segregated and separated track events intolerable. He and his friend C. C. Jackson petitioned the authorities in Baltimore to relieve the segregated practices in athletics and give the colored athletes an opportunity to compete on a more reasonable basis. Their persistence and determination, along with the support they were able to bring to bear against the practice, proved successful.

Many black athletes today who have achieved fame in track, football, or the Olympics have never heard of the 5'8", 140.pound All American named Eddie Hurt. Eddie's intellect, determination, and dignity helped to open many closed doors for black athletes, but Eddie was so modest and unassuming that many people did not realize his gifts.

It is difficult to describe the intensity of the man, but many athletes will tell you that his sinister stare and that nervous pacing with his hands in his pocket as he half walked or half jogged toward them almost froze them in their tracks.

Alphonso Cottman, class of 1931, says he never broke 50 seconds in the quarter mile until Eddie asked him "why he was so slow." The next day during a time trial (another Hurt peculiarity), Cottman was burning around the first turn and had started the back stretch where he settled into his usual long stride, or float, as quarter milers called it (a kind of relaxed means of running where speed is not necessarily reduced but needless motion is reduced and oxygen is not burned as fast). But right at the middle of the stretch, he heard Coach Hurt yell, "Run from there!" He was so startled that he burst into an all-out sprint, down the backstretch, around the turn and up the final leg. Cottman hit the tape and Eddie Hurt was there with three watches, another trademark. All of them had Cottman at 49 seconds; he was the first Morgan man to break the 50-second quarter mile barrier. If Chuck Yeager thinks breaking the sound barrier was significant, it couldn't compare to the whooping and hollering that was going on that day. Cottman was so elated that he ran over to Coach and grabbed him, looking for a word of congratulations. Eddie looked at him, put his hands in his pockets, and said; "Now we go to work!"

Perhaps that incident did more than anything else to elevate Eddie and the Bears to world-renowned fame. "Run from there" became a Morgan battle cry. That cry somehow became part of the athlete. It didn't stop at the edge of the athletic field or the basketball court, but every Morgan man will tell you it meant "give it all you've got" no matter what the situation. One of Eddie's quarter milers, Robert "Billy" Thompson, out of Atlanta, Georgia, once said that Eddie told him to "let nothing break your stride." This thought enabled him to overcome adversities and disappointments later in his professional life. Thompson says that Eddie was a compassionate person as well as a diplomat. It seems that Thompson reported for football practice, but Eddie knew he would not last long around the Morgan Bears. Eddie began to borrow his football uniform piece by piece until Thompson became confused. That afternoon he went to see Mom Hurt. She took one look at him and cried out, "Boy get away from there, they'll break every bone in your little body". As Thompson puts it today, "she saved me from the mighty Conrad, Wilson, and Clark."

Eddie demonstrated his tact and intellect again in Philadelphia back in 1931 when he took his team to the Penn relays. They stopped to eat in a Philadelphia restaurant but couldn't get served. Eddie called his wife Beatrice and explained the situation to her. After a long and somewhat bitter conversation with her, he turned his anger around and used tact and diplomacy in a way that protected the team's well being. He chose to find another place to eat and remain in Philadelphia to allow his team to participate in the relays.

CHAPTER I

THE GROWING YEARS

The '30s were growing years. Eddie had begun to develop his own coaching techniques. It was natural for him to insist on hard work from his athletes. After all, he could remember the many years he had labored on his father's 275-acre farm near Brookneal, Virginia: an area where tobacco, corn, and wheat had for many years been the major crops. The bright sun and long days in the tobacco fields taught him the value of honest effort and toil. He learned to identify the loafers quickly. His apt and agile mind, fine-tuned by many years of concentration on his major field, mathematics, helped him to sort out the men from the boys.

During those early years, there were some strong football teams. The old-timers still tell about the powerhouse teams from Howard, Shaw, and Lincoln Universities. In those days, coaching was done by the older and more experienced players or by some members of the faculty. Victory was all-important. Defeat was looked upon as a disgrace and as something to be avoided by any and every means possible.

Those days, one hardly expected to witness a contest without having it prematurely end by some untoward circumstance. Zealous spectators often interfered with the progress of the game if their team was losing. In rare instances, fans were known to tackle runners who had gotten away for a touchdown. One case is remembered where an end recovered a fumbled punt and was on his way to a touchdown when a spectator ran onto the field of play near the goal line with a board and dared the runner to cross the goal line!

The early '30s were big years for Morgan, and Eddie was so busy that even Bea, his beautiful young wife, seldom saw him. When pressed, he would say that his strongest fan was Bea. As Hurt put it, "She frequently criticizes my plays and tells me when I am wrong – not publicly, but privately." Eddie called Bea the finest woman in the world. There are many others who will testify to her beauty and character. Today, Bea has beautiful silver hair covering an exquisitely sculptured ebony face of obvious royal origin. Throughout the years, great numbers of young men and women have sought her help and guidance. Many would call and speak with "Mom" Hurt prior to ever speaking with Coach. Eddie had a tendency to sit quietly and chuckle because he knew they were in the best hands. On one occasion "Mom" Hurt received a phone call from a young freshman who had come to Morgan in hopes of earning a track scholarship. Coach had called for time trials on the very day the young man had reported to the school infirmary with the Flu. He ran the time trial and not only finished last but had the slowest time. Dejected, he was preparing to go back to the Virginia tobacco fields. A friend suggested calling "Mom" Hurt and tell her the story. That night she prepared coach's supper and sat quietly. Coach noticed this behavior and asked her if there was a problem. Bea spoke up, "Why are your time trials like the Last Supper – life or death." Eddie almost choked on his food. He smiled when he spoke of that situation. It seems she helped him to discover his new anchorman for the mile relay and the CIAA championship.

Hurt met Bea when she arrived at Virginia Seminary as a teacher. He said when he saw her, he had only one game plan, and as history demonstrated, "she caught him." It seems that Eddie had developed a plan or strategy to attract her attention. He knew what Bea's daily teaching schedule was, and he would always place himself somewhere along the path that she walked. When Bea passed by, Eddie would say "Good Morning." Bea would sometimes reply but seldom look his way. One day, she turned and looked at him, smiled and said, "Good Morning." Eddie remembers that day as one of his best. As time passed and Bea remained cordial, Eddie developed a new plan. He learned about a faculty dance that Bea was planning to attend. He had never danced, so he hired someone to teach him. This was successful. However, as Coach explained, he used up all his lunch money to learn.

It was not long afterwards that Eddie decided to ask for Bea's hand in marriage. He explained that for the first time in his life, his confidence level registered zero. But this one thing he knew was that he loved that "Lady". It would have been easier to accept three technical fouls on the basketball court or maybe two twenty yard penalties on the football field. But, if she said "No", he knew his world would have crumbled. Fortunately, when he quietly approached her and asked for her hand, she said, "Yes".

Eddie married G. Beatrice Reid on August 31, 1922 in a wedding that was described as beautiful and serene. The couple had to postpone honeymoon plans and leave immediately for Lynchburg, Virginia. Eddie was under contract to start coaching and teaching at Virginia Seminary.

Beatrice had a teaching certificate from Cheney State Teaching College, and she had planned on a teaching career. However, it was not until Eddie moved to Morgan State College that she was able to complete her degree. Cheney did not offer the Bachelors Degree.

The young couple found the early years tough, for Eddie's salary hardly paid for a place to live. She remembers that they ate their dinners in the school dinning hall.

During the summer months, the two would head for New York where Bea's family lived. Eddie found work at the train station as a "Red Cap". Bea found work as a waitress, many times not getting home for a week at a time. She remembers the time as happy ones with Eddie.

A wise man once said that behind every great man is a greater woman. Eddie Hurt would appreciate my using that over worked phrase because he quoted it often. What he meant was that if any good came to him, it was because of Bea. She was his inspiration. Mom Hurt is a woman of great understanding, wisdom, and love. Those about her sense a powerful presence, an aura of peace and tranquility. Eddie cherished her and lived daily knowing that he could depend on and find sanctuary within his loving home with her. Not one day passed that Eddie didn't consult her. She was in fact his confidante, his source of peace in turmoil, his understanding companion in times of strife and confusion. He learned that whatever the situation, whether football, basketball, or people, she knew the answer, and he would consult her first. Mom had sat in the stands at football games, traveled to distant schools to observe basketball games and at night, over simple meals, they talked.

The entire University community became aware of this jewel on their campus. Presently, Mom Hurt is highly revered and honored. Her honors include: Founders Award M.S.U. for Leadership and Service; President's Club M.S.U. Foundation Inc. for Leadership in Education; Hall of Fame M.S.U. Alumni Association for Outstanding Service; Proclamation 20 years of Service M.S.U. A Day in Honor of Beatrice Hurt; The City Council of Baltimore, Meritorious Service Award; Congressional Achievement Award for Dedication and Commitment to the Community; Meritorious Service Award M.S.U. National Alumni Association Class of 1949; Honorary Member 50th Anniversary Club Life Study Fellowships with an additional four (4) certificates of appreciation from organizations for service and leadership. The Social Security Administration; The Citizens for a Drug Free America; The National Children's Cancer Society; The National Parks Service and the American with Disabilities Organization.

Bea was Hurt's devoted wife until the day he died on March 24, 1989. She cared for his every need and even catalogued all of his accomplishments. She is a source of inspiration and leadership on Morgan's campus as witnessed by her honors. Besides supporting all the athletes through their trials and tribulations, she developed a solid core of benefactors to assist in scholarships and grants. She still attends meetings to insure that funds are available for the hardship students. She also maintains a leadership role in helping to guide her beloved sorority Alpha Kappa Alpha, to achieve its goals. The two grew gracefully together, and their home was serene and united. Perhaps that's why the "boys" return again and again.

The Bears won three consecutive CIAA Conference basketball championships, keeping stride with the football team. Eddie, many observers will tell you, could spot an athlete walking on the other side of the campus 400 yards away. Before the student would know what had happened, Eddie had him either jogging, jumping, or shooting baskets. He would tell the young student, "I'll see you this August at football (or basketball) practice!" Some observers reported that many of his players thought it was a mandatory three-credit course. He could take raw talent and mold it until the final product was a refined athlete.

The basketball team was drilled daily. Eddie insisted upon set offense and defensive patterns – no backyard one-on-one. Basketball, as Hurt saw it, was a game that required teamwork and skill. He later was quoted as saying, "coaching is an art."

Like an artist, a coach will mentally sketch the idea of a play that he wants to develop in his mind. In Eddie's mind, basketball was more like a great ballet where each man had intricate maneuvers to perform around a sphere called a basketball, and where timing was all-important. If it was properly executed, Eddie could see the mathematical relationship of picks, passes, and screens. He told one reporter, "Mathematics is an aid to coaching football and basketball. It helps in timing and diagramming of plays." In addition, Eddie felt a good coach has to be a dreamer. He has to see possibilities in his mind and then be able to take the abstract and make a mold of flesh and blood into its likeness.

Bea recalls that one time she gave Eddie a letter to mail. When she failed to receive a reply within a reasonable time, she became suspicious. After talking with "Hurt," as she referred to him, she discovered that he had diagrammed a play on the letter and forgotten to mail it. She went on to explain that it was common to find plays diagrammed on books, napkins, tablecloths, and some of her finest linens.

Hurt and his friend and colleague Marse Hill were always on time and ahead of their contemporaries. Perhaps some insight into the great devotion Eddie had for the game can be illuminated by the following. He and Hill would travel almost anywhere to attend a football or basketball clinic, sometimes sharing a peanut butter sandwich and a flask of coffee prepared by Bea. The two had hardly enough money to provide the gas for Hill's father's 1930 Buick.

The walls of Eddie's den were covered with plaques attesting to the coaching seminars and clinics that he and Hill attended. Most notable is one dated 1935, Northeastern University Coaching School, certifying their attendance at the coaching clinic headed up by the following football greats:
Frank Thomas - University of Alabama; Dr. J. B. Sutherland – University of Pittsburgh; Richard C. Harlow – Harvard University; Andrew Kerr – Colgate University; Harley W. Anderson – North Carolina State College; Joseph C. McKenney

– Boston College; Paul D. Hinkle – Boston University (basketball training); and Henry J. Kontoff – Northern University. Eddie was doing his homework under the finest names in the game.

With such a voracious appetite for the finer points of the game, Eddie's game plans were always detailed in graphic displays with his own special insight and adaptations to the single-wing or "T" formation.

He never left things to chance. They not only taught burning the midnight oil to their students, they practiced the same. Burning the midnight oil was a trademark of his and Hill's.

Hill, a legend in his own right (The Hill Field House on Morgan's campus was named in his honor) as a basketball/football coach, completely complemented Hurt's talents. Hill taught an 8:00 a.m. health education class to all freshman. He was revered on the campus because he insisted that all students learn the value of health education, and also the value of being on time. Whenever a student was late for Coach Hill's class, he would look at the student and calmly say, "Sorry money, the train has left." The student had no choice but to turn around and leave.

Campus of Morgan State University

The year 1931 saw Hurt's Bears win 4 games and lose 2. They lost the last game of the season 26-0 to Hampton Institute, who won the CIAA Championship that year. From that last loss of 1931, Hurt's Elevens achieved one of the most impressive string of victories ever achieved by a collegiate team.

Reporter Sam Lacy has pointed out that in the years preceding the Negroes' advent on the major league baseball scene, sports observers voiced a standard lament. Every time they saw the great Negro ball player Josh Gibson of the Homestead Grays clout a home run over Pittsburgh's Forbes field centerfield wall, or Satchel Paige pitch a shut-out, or Oscar Charleston make a nifty catch in the outfield, they would begin "If he were only white…" The idea was that had any of these players (and others) been paler of face, they most certainly would have been major league stars.

"There weren't as many laments of this type in football, because Negroes began playing the rougher sport in predominantly white colleges before the turn of the century and they were on hand for the birth of pro football, continuing as stars until 1931, when a

15-year old Jim-Crow movement began; the lull ended in 1946 when the now defunct All American Conference displayed colored players" (Sam Lacy, Baltimore Afro-American Newspaper). Yet today, as much as one might dislike to use it, nothing is more significant in speaking of Edward Hurt than that old lament. If Eddie had been given a chance to coach at Notre Dame, Southern California, or Alabama there is little doubt that he would now be ranked alongside the likes of Knute Rockne, Pop Warner, and Alonzo Stagg.

Morgan State College Football Squad
1937 National CIAA Champions

Morgan State, after the last defeat by Hampton Institute in 1931, didn't lose another game until 1938. During that period, Hurt's teams went 54 games without one defeat. In that string were 47 triumphs and 7 ties. That record rivals the 1901-1905 mark posted by that famous Michigan point-a-minute team of "Hurry-up" Yost, which boasted 55 victories and one loss. Eddie's teams scored 1,179 points to the opponents' 94. They were tied 7 times, but no team could beat them. In fact, the 1933 team was so powerful that Eddie referred to it until he died as one of his greatest Elevens. They scored 398 points while holding their opponents to a mere touchdown. This team produced the Morgan-famous "Four Horsemen": Conrad, Wilson, Troupe, and Sturgis.

Johnny Sturgis of Harrisburg, Pennsylvania was halfback on the football team and also a member of the track team, known for his excellent physical conditioning. He was the best open field runner in Morgan history, a cutback artist and all-around triple-threat man. His cutback style of running fit Eddie's offensive attack perfectly since Eddie was already using "trap" blocking.

Otis "What-a-Man" Troupe of New Jersey was an all CIAA selection and an All-American selection. Many considered him to be the best of the Four Horsemen, but that argument will never be settled.

Brutus Wilson, also of New Jersey, was quarterback and mastermind of the Four Horsemen. An all-around athlete, he also helped captain the 1934 CIAA basketball championship team. Brutus was a master ball handler, and whenever Eddie talked about his offense, he would say that although it was not "T" formation, one thing he was sure of was that Brutus would have been a great "T" formation quarterback. Brutus graduated from Morgan and became head coach of Winston-Salem and later head coach at Shaw University.

Thomas "Tank" Conrad was the workhorse of the backfield. "Tank" seldom attempted to run around a would-be tackler; he just lowered his shoulder and ran over most men. Running out of Eddie's offensive patterns, Troupe and Conrad were known to return to the huddle and badger Brutus the quarterback about which play to call next. Both men loved to carry the ball, but Eddie Hurt's offensive plays always called for each man to be effective in the play. In most cases, they were blocking ahead of the ball carrier or assigned a downfield blocking pattern. Both men realized that blocking was important, but there was glory in carrying the ball. Usually, Brutus would ignore both men and call the play he thought best, or wait for Coach to send in the next play. When that occurred, it inevitably resulted in Morgan scoring again.

THE FAMED FOUR HORSEMEN

Widely heralded as one of the greatest backfields ever produced by the Hurt-Hill combination was this foursome: (left to right) Otis Troupe, fullback; Tom (Tank) Conrad, left half: John Sturgis, right half: Brutus Wilson, quarterback.

At the 23rd Annual Meeting of the CIAA, Eddie Hurt, as a result of his recent championship, was called upon to speak. In his soft, unassuming style, he explained to the audience how to develop a strong offensive football team. His basic premise was that there are many problems which must be solved. He selected five of these as a basis for his argument.

1. The problem of the qualifications of a coach in the offensive phase of the games.
2. The problem of the development of the physical condition of the squad.
3. The problems of teaching the fundamentals of offensive plays.
4. The problem of the selection of a system that best fits the personnel of the squad.
5. The problem of offensive generalship.

When he completed his lecture on the above subjects, he had captivated his audience. This was his gift, the ability to see analytically through a problem and plan strategies spontaneously to overcome the situation.

Eddie Hurt was much like a field general trained at West Point or at Sandhurst. He could see his opposing force's strengths and weaknesses. He had no eyes or ears up front in the battlefield to inform him of the enemy's movement, no screening force or forward observers, for such scouting capabilities had not yet reached the budgets of the CIAA Conference members, much less Morgan's meager budget. So without the benefit of scouts, Eddie often had to adopt a wait-and-see attitude, and then he adjusted, utilizing the skills that his team either possessed or did not possess.

Richard "Red" Roberts of Baltimore, Maryland, recalls those early days with Coach Hurt. Playing as a lineman on the squad, Red recalls the long, hard drills which often left him battered and bruised. But to this day, if you ask Red, he will tell you that Hurt not only made him a better athlete, but he also taught him lessons that have assisted him throughout life.

Red produced this chart:

ASSIGNMENTS FOR LEFT GUARD

PLAY	6 MAN LINE	7 MAN LINE
14, 24, 34, 64, 16, 26, 66, 76, 18, 28	Lead play	Lead play
12	Thru for center	Guard
16, 17, 25, 23, 27, 33, 73, 65	Guard	Guard
31	Half back	Full back
32	Mouse trap defensive left guard	
74	Mouse trap defensive left tackle	
63	Defensive right tackle	
75	Help end on defensive right tackle	
All "x" plays same as straight play assignments		
41, 42	Out left block tackle and end	
43, 86	Out left to take tackle	
44, 40, 47	Out left and take end	
46	Out right and block tackle	
Shift to left
End Run
Off tackle
Reverse

Half back
Guard
Lead play |

Guard
Guard
Lead play |

CHAPTER II

THE WAR YEARS

The 1940s started with the ominous clouds of war facing the world. The gloom touched every part of this small planet. It is doubtful that any college conference escaped the loss of first class talent, as the country started its mobilization. The professional leagues suspended their schedules or reduced levels of competition.

In the early '40s, young men were being drafted into the services in such numbers that many colleges suspended their athletic schedules. The CIAA was seriously affected; in some cases, schools curtailed all of their inter-collegiate competition.

Coach Hurt and Marse Hill continued their philosophy of never quitting, and they put together some excellent teams. It is difficult to evaluate the degree of success since the opposition was also weakened by the draft.

Morgan State College found itself struggling during the 1939 season, and as a result, had already slipped into the Conference's second division. Hurt found himself in an extremely unfamiliar situation. His team was beaten, and raw new talent was hard to find. However, Hurt the coach/philosopher never let the situation dictate his options.

Approaching the mid '40s, only 8 of 14 CIAA members were able to field football teams.

Prior to discussing Morgan's athletic program, there are some notable editorials and speeches, which relate to the Conference as a whole.

The Conference leadership had a great desire to promote wholesome athletic competition among its members. The author believes that the groundwork laid in the early '40s was characterized by extreme foresight and wisdom by some of the most far-thinking black men of the era.

The CIAA, in its 1940 bulletin, opened with this editorial:

>A WORD ABOUT THE C.I.A.A.
>Journal & Guide (Editorial, 1-20-40)

>"We think it appropriate to say a word of praise for one of Negro America's finest organizations, the Colored Intercollegiate Athletic Association. This important body, which governs the athletic activities of the thirteen outstanding colleges of the East, has a complex and difficult job, but it discharges its responsibility with a maximum of ease and efficiency. Its most recent annual meeting at AT&T College in Greensboro showed the conference at its best.

>When the representatives of 13 colleges, all concerned with their own interests, can be molded together into a group which can decide important issues in such a way as to yield the best for Negro college athletics, at times sacrificing advantages that might accrue to each separately, then a splendid and commendable job has been done by those unselfish men who founded and developed the C.I.A.A.

>This organization is the oldest such Negro conference in the United States and has set the standards by which all of the others have patterned themselves."

Dr. Rufus E. Clement, President of Atlanta University in 1940, speaking at the same conference, emphasized even more the role of the CIAA. An excerpt from his speech entitled "The Brighter Side of College Athletics":

"I want to talk with you for a few minutes on the brighter side of college athletics.

I can remember my first football game somewhere in the early 1900s. I watched a football game on the campus of Biddle University, now Johnson C. Smith, on Thanksgiving Day. Biddle University and Livingstone College played the first college football game between Negro colleges in America. I watched the game, as a mere lad, wondering what the men were fighting about.

Let me begin by admitting that everything is not as it should be in the college for Negroes. Let me also tell you that the college for Negroes is no wise guilty of many of these charges, as many of our other American colleges are. We have not gone to the extremes to which other institutions have been charged. We have not spent hundreds of thousands of dollars for great stadiums – no, we have not paid board, room, tuition, and salary. We have not made our coaches more important than our faculty members. The tramp athlete in Negro colleges has been driven into obscurity. Some twenty years ago or more a man might this year play with a particular college; next year he could play with another, and if you did not watch out, the man who helped you beat college "A" last year would help college "A" beat you.

In this conference you have helped in raising the academic standards for all the students. In this conference, you have set a minimum of academic achievement, which must be met before an individual is eligible to play on a team. There is a story told about a great American athlete who a few years ago was playing his last football game. He had played a magnificent game that day. He had aided his team to defeat their opposition. The coach, knowing this was his last game, took the man out of the game thirty seconds before it was over so the crowd could give him the ovation, which he had earned. Tears were pouring down his cheeks as he was going blindly to the dressing room; a sports writer met him and asked him what he was crying about. The athlete, with tears coming down his cheeks said, 'This is my last game, and I would be much happier today if during these four years I had learned how to read.' I say that day has gone forever."

What does this have to do with Eddie Hurt? In order to help the reader understand the man, some of the pressures that he encountered during the early years of his training can provide background. The CIAA was geared for the highest standard of athletic competition and scholarship. Eddie was a man and coach who stood for the highest ideas of fair play, integrity, and decency.

You will not find the slightest scandal or misuse of a student athlete. Eddie enjoyed pointing out that over 90 percent of his athletes graduated and went on to greater things in life. He could name doctors, lawyers, educators, college presidents, military officers, ministers, bishops, and publishers as just a few of the many who obtained prominence.

At the start of the 1939 football season, Eddie found his Bears slipping. For the first time in more than 10 years, Morgan was placed in the second division. Teams like North Carolina A&T College and Virginia State College, the defending 1939 champions, were big and strong. Morgan's team was an unknown factor. They had a strong offense, but for some reason the team failed to score many points when near the goal line. Most of their games were lost by close scores; nevertheless, they lost.

In basketball, Eddie's 1940 team won seven and lost five. The CIAA used the Dickinson rating system which awarded points according to the number of victories over first and second division teams. For example, Virginia Union and North Carolina both won 14 Conference games each; however, Union received

27.22 points to North Carolina's 26.25 points due to more victories over first division teams than second division teams. Therefore, Union was declared the Conference champions. By this time, most of the Conference play was characterized by intricate fast-break offenses and airtight zone and man-to-man defense. The league as a whole was playing a better game of basketball, practically on a level with top collegiate basketball. It was faster, ball handling and passing were of high caliber, and as a result, attendance records were broken as fans eagerly watched the fiery competition.

In track, Eddie continued to build superb men, and the Bears performed well at the two Conference-sponsored meets: The CIAA Open Meet at A&T College, and the CIAA Championship Meet at Hampton Institute.

On May 11, 1940 at the CIAA Open Track Meet, the fans were treated to a great spectacle. The great Olympian and American favorite, Jesse Owens, made a personal appearance. Jesse made a few short remarks and then acted as starter for a special exhibition 880-yard run by "Long John" Woodruff, Olympic 800-meter champion, and John Borican, National Pentathlon and 1,000-yard champion. Long John Woodruff won the race by inches as Borican closed in at the tape. During the race, Jesse Owens treated the fans by describing the two different styles of running by the two great runners.

Eddie's men scored 20 points that day, but not enough to match powerful Virginia State with 56 points, and Hampton's 31.

The Hurt & Hill combination came back strong in the years 1940 and 1941, winning the Conference football championship both years. Most impressive was the manner in which the Bears played, using an offense built around deception and speed-- Hurt's trademark. In a lecture during the early '40s, he emphasized the need for proper execution of fundamentals and the necessity of having a number of plays start the same way but end differently, what many today might refer to as misdirection plays. This was deception at its best, and Hurt went on to illustrate this type of offense, which he thought offered the best chance for success.

Professor H. C. Perrin, President of Shaw University, in his speech to the 28th Annual Meeting of the CIAA in 1941, referred to the excellent work of Hurt and Hill by congratulating them for a wonderful football team, and continued by praising all of the coaches on the overall upgrading of the CIAA football. Needless to say, Hurt influenced many of the CIAA teams. It has to be remembered that Eddie was coaching not only football and basketball, but also wrestling, tennis, and boxing.

The Morgan "Bears"
1944 Team

(#47: "Big House" Gaines, #19: "Boo" Brown, #48: "Tippy" Day, #52: Leonard Ford)

In a 1945 CIAA bulletin, Eddie wrote an article called "Football in the CIAA."

FOOTBALL IN THE CIAA
E.P. Hurt

Director of Physical Education, Morgan State College

"Football in the Colored Intercollegiate Athletic Association in 1944 managed to keep afloat in spite of tremendous handicaps and hardships, brought about by a world at war that threatened to engulf it. Only eight of the fourteen members were able to put teams on the gridiron. The Conference, however, takes pride in the belief that it is doing a small part on the home front in bolstering morale and in giving at least some mental diversion for those who are carrying the ball in that all-important game on foreign field.

All the colleges had to rely entirely upon limited civilian personnel that made it difficult for any of the coaches to turn out a really first class team. However, there was no lack of competition among the group. Taking their cues from the generals on the fighting fronts who made 1944 a year of attack, the coaches stressed their offenses and allowed their defenses to take care of themselves. The T-formation was still very much in evidence, but inexperienced personnel forced some colleges to go back to the single wing attack."

Morgan State College Bears and the highly rated Virginia State College Trojans battled it out in Petersburg, Virginia on Thanksgiving Day 1944, with the Conference championship at stake. The Morgan Bears had a stubborn opponent to handle but came from behind to take this one, 6-3, and the Championship along with it. The defeat of the highly favored Virginia State team in the Thanksgiving Day Classic was described by Hurt in an article published by the Baltimore *Afro-American* in 1944:

By Edward P. Hurt
(Head Coach at Morgan College)

"Baltimore – The secret of Morgan's surprising and convincing rout of the highly favored Virginia State team in the Thanksgiving Day Classic here two weeks ago is really no secret at all. It was simple, and had our opponents applied themselves to the situation, we might not have got away with it. But, we beat them with a five-man line, and that's it. The way I look at it, we outsmarted them and played to their weaknesses, using a five-man line defense as the ace in the hole."

Explains System

"Here's how: State would have the ball. Morgan would line up with the regular seven-line in a 7-1-2-1 defensive formation. However, in the split second before the ball was snapped, Morgan would drop two of its linesmen back, usually a guard and center. This left five men on the line with an almost doubled increase in the secondary defense.

There were two reasons for this split second shifting. First, the main objective was to confuse the State offense and blockers. Each man on an offensive team has his work cut out for him. He is supposed to block a certain opponent or opponents. After the huddle, State would line up and find our men in one position. Then just before the ball was snapped, we dropped two men to the backfield, thus making it considerably more difficult for opposing blockers to find their man or men.

Our second reason for using a five-man line to the seven was because we were scared of their Aces, Bailey and Briscoe. That's it, we were plenty scared. I know what those two could do and how they could wiggle their way many yards even after they have been hit solidly."

Took No Chances

"We wouldn't take any chances. A five-man line is weaker than a seven, but on the other hand, our secondary was strengthened. Bailey, especially, is adept at slashing his way through any team's first line defense. If the secondary is not on its toes and does not have the necessary defense, he is gone for a touchdown anytime.

Hence our strengthened secondary. If he or any of the other slippery State backs got past our first line, we had a second shot and were sure not to miss this second time.

We had our safety play back just far enough to stop any run that might have gotten past our first two lines of defense. This 5-3-2-1 defense paid its reward in big dividends.

Then again, State's coaching staff used single wingbacks in all offensive plays. That system is terribly easy to diagnose. We figured if we had the strength, it would be simple, as every man on our squad knew just about every trick in State's little bag. It was a matter of recognizing each play in that split second after the ball had been snapped."

Didn't Have A Chance

"Most times we did. That's how it was that most of the time our boys would be through State's line and smothering the ball runner before he could get under way.

In other words all during practice, for weeks, we worked and worked on defense. We knew our offense. It was defense we stressed. Our boys were properly keyed for the game. We held prayer meetings and pep talks and testimonials.

When we took the field on Thanksgiving Day, we KNEW we were ready. One minute after the game began we KNEW State wasn't ready. That was just what we wanted. It was a simple matter of playing to the other fellow's weakness after that, letting no opportunity slip by. The rest is already known.

And that's the real secret of how Morgan beat State!"

The Morgan Bears had another good season with "Tippy" Day and Freddie Burgess, the Conference's most valuable player, as backfield standouts, and with Clarence "Big House" Gaines, Charlie Frazier, and Leonard Ford as the big men up front. It should be noted that Leonard Ford is the same athlete that went on to great fame as a member of the National Football League's Cleveland Browns. Clarence "Big House" Gaines went on to become one of America's greatest coaches and educators at Winston-Salem College in North Carolina.

While Hurt stressed the fact that the war caused a recruitment problem, the coaches continued to improve their offensive and defensive patterns. On defense, there was an occasional 6-3-2 and a 5-man line as the tactical situation dictated.

Their only defeat was by the Tuskegee Army Air Force, a strong service team. Morgan won the Conference crown for the fifth successive time and remained undefeated in colleges' circles since the middle of the 1942 season.

In light of the above, it should be noted that Hurt's 1943 football team went undefeated, untied, and unscored upon; the 1946 team also was undefeated and untied.

In June of 1947, at the Third Annual Florida A&M College Football Clinic, Eddie was one of the featured lecturers. He lectured on modern approach to football offenses: T-formation with unbalanced line; single-wing requirements; fundamental running plays T-formation; and training and conditioning.

One alumnus and former bear football player, John M. Williams Jr. of Baltimore, Maryland, remembers those years and teams of the '40s as some of Morgan's finest. In the National Classic held in Washington, D.C., in 1943, the Bears walloped Florida A&M 50-0. In 1946, the Bears ran over Grambling College 33-0. At that time, the great Eddie Robinson, coach of Grambling, had been at the school only six years. Williams remembers that the great "Tank" Younger was on that Grambling team. He recalls such talent as Clarence "Big House" Gaines and Alvin "Boo" Brown, along with Joe Black of Brooklyn Dodgers fame, Oscar Givens, Terry Day, Art Fauntleroy, Roy Cragway, and others on the early 1940s teams.

Some of the "old guys" remember Hurt's tactics in those days as extremely tough and exhausting. It seems many veterans were returning from the military in early 1946. Hurt decided to weed out his team early. Two weeks prior to the first scheduled practice, he and Hill had two 60-minute scrimmages on successive days. After those two scrimmages, there was no doubt who would play.

It's interesting to note that Eddie's former players have the same recollections: Hurt demanded discipline — penalties for jumping offside and holding were dealt with in practice, usually through scrimmages. If you wanted to play ball, you had to learn Hurt's system. Most plays were misdirected with usually two blockers on one.

Clarence "Big House" Gaines (today a legend in his own right at Winston-Salem College) was one of Hurt's most cherished athletes. He refers to Hurt as a brilliant, astute tactician. He credits Hurt, as do most of Hurt's men, with providing him with more than just athletic opportunity. He learned basic life philosophies, to think, to fight, to win, to never give up, to "run from there." These were things a young black man facing life in the '30s, '40s, and '50s needed to cope with, in order to survive the American society's early social philosophy. Gaines recalls one moment during a basketball game that the Bears were 15 points down. He told Hurt, "Don't worry about it until we do!" As Gaines remembers it, Hurt yelled, "You guys don't have enough damn sense to know when to get worried!" Gaines says no one else recalls Hurt ever using such language.

Coaches of the "Bears" Morgan State College
Alvin Brown, Edward P. Hurt, Talmadge L. Hill, and Kenneth Brown

Along with Gaines was another one of Hurt's protégés, Alvin "Boo" Brown, 1941-45. Brown was another super athlete years ahead of his time. A two-letter man, Brown played with Gaines on some great championship teams, but he credits Hurt with taking a small-town boy and developing his athletic skills until it amazed even him. Because he had all of the skills necessary to be a good coach, and the ability to handle men, Hurt recruited Brown as an assistant coach almost immediately after graduation. His specialty was training the backfield players whom he kept finely tuned. He coached the Morgan teams from 1945-1946 and later 1951-56. Members of the backfield remember him as a perfectionist and taskmaster with the tenacity of an army bootcamp training sergeant as he executed the plays drawn up by Coach Hurt. Under Coach Hurt, Brown captained the Morgan Bears to the CIAA Basketball Championship in 1945. Together they were a real force in the basketball arena. Brown was a scholar athlete. He enrolled at Columbia University and received a master's degree in physical education, then he coached for short stints at Winston-Salem Teachers College, North Carolina and Arkansas State prior to returning to his alma mater in the early

1950s to resume coaching. He remained with Hurt until the call to greater achievements lured him away to medical school at Meharry, where he graduated as an MD. He credits Hurt and his wife, "Mom" Hurt, as his guiding lights. He explains that Eddie was decades ahead of his coaching peers, in developing various blocking techniques, play design, and game plans.

Hurt's analytical ability was a gift, and he used it to take advantage of his opponent's strengths to turn them into weaknesses. During one game in Greensboro in 1952, playing against the contending national champions, North Carolina A&T, Eddie took a mediocre team and beat the powerful Aggies. Hurt was known to pull off some truly amazing wins just when his team was made a solid underdog.

Eddie Hurt was a serious individual, and during one half time when the Bears were 12 points down against West Virginia State, in an attempt to motivate them, he furiously kicked a box. Unfortunately, his foot stuck in the box. Brown says, "No one cracked even a smile."

The 1940s ended as dramatically as they had begun. Hurt's eleventh CIAA football championship came with his 1949 super powerhouse team, which was undefeated and scored 226 points to the opponents' 33. Hurt was close to becoming a legend at this point. When questioned about comparisons between the 1949 team and the 1946 and 1933 teams, he became somewhat diplomatic and refused to comment, choosing to leave it to history.

There are those who like to point to Eddie Hurt with pride and refer to him as "the grand old man of coaching," but his favorite pastime was always enjoying the accomplishments of his boys both on and off the track, gridiron or court. When pressed for the reason for his success, he would point to Marse Hill or his other assistant coaches, or even mumble something about luck. But those closest to him, notably his devoted wife, Bea, will tell you that Eddie was gifted to know and understand men. His judgment was unerring.

Besides "Boo" Brown, Hurt selected as his other assistant coach another of his students, Kenneth E. Brown. Kenneth, a Morgan Star on the 1938-39 and 1940 football teams was a highly regarded athlete and astute Hurt disciple. He was the assistant line coach and also coached wrestling and boxing.

Eddie continued to coach basketball from 1929 to 1947. During that time, his Cagers won four CIAA championships. After that, Marse Hill took over the head basketball coaching position, giving Hurt more time to work as athletic director and head football and track coach.

Eddie contributed the following article to the CIAA in 1945:

Basketball in the
Colored Intercollegiate Athletic Association for 1945

By E. P. Hurt
Director of Physical Education, Morgan State College

"The teams in the Colored Intercollegiate Athletic Association displayed an interesting type of basketball during the 1945 season. Although hard hit by graduation and by inductions into the various branches of the armed forces, the teams battled each other all the way to the wire.

The defensive systems employed by the competing teams were almost equally divided between the many kinds of zones and the traditional man-to-man defense. The conference champions and the third place teams used zones in most of their games. The offense followed the modern style of fast-breaking, free-shooting basketball. Against man-to-man defenses, the offense usually sent one or two pivot men inside while the outside men maneuvered in a figure eight formation.
Morgan State College won the conference crown for the first time in twelve years. The 'Bears' were a hard-hitting, perpetual motion team that rolled through fifteen

conference games without a defeat. Lanky Lennie Ford did a good job on the backboards. "Dickey" Burke and "Tippy" Day kept the ball moving and Cal Irvin and "Boo" Brown excelled at putting the ball into the basket. The high point of their season was the two victories over the high-flying North Carolina College "Eagles." North Carolina College with Stanley and Thomas carrying the weight, lost only to Morgan State and ended their season in the runner-up spot."

Elmore Pepper Harris
400 meter National Champion

Bob Tyler
National Junior 100/200 meter Champion

Byron Labatch
Morgan Sprinter, Olympian - Jamaican National Team

CHAPTER III

THE 1950s NATIONAL AND INTERNATIONAL ACCLAIM

The 1950s came in like a tornado. Eddie Hurt was reaching the peak of his capabilities as a coach. Morgan football, track under Hurt, and basketball under Marsh Hill were reaching great heights. Hurt was more determined than ever to produce quality athletes and to break down the walls of racial bias in the sports world to demonstrate that his teams were capable of competing with the schools of the NCAA. He accomplished this task, but in a unique way.

This quote from the address given by President John H. Burr at the 36th Annual Meeting of the CIAA in 1949 points out the feelings and the activities of the black colleges in that period:

> "For the first time, we have been able to get many more interracial games than we have played before. This movement is being fostered not only from within but from without. The American Physical Education Association has formed a committee that is entitled the 'Intergroup and Intercultural Committee' whose function is to try to promote better interracial relationships through physical education and athletics.
>
> I have the honor to serve on that committee and I want to urge at this time that we cooperate with this movement by being acceptable to the principles and the plans that they are promoting, and further that we will expect to make as many advances to our friends of the other race as they make to us.

During the year, Lincoln and Howard perhaps have been leading along this particular line. Other schools, such as Hampton, have played many institutions. Among the schools that we have played this year have been Bergen, Lock Haven Teachers College, Brooklyn College, Seton Hall, the University of Maryland, Oberlin, McGill, and others too numerous to name. In each one of these contests, it has been mentioned that not only have they enjoyed the competition with our teams, but also the fellowship and social benefits that are derived from a program of this type.

I want to congratulate the men of the Association who are doing this work and trust that the rest of us will get on the train to help this movement along.

During the year we attended the N.C.A.A. meeting in New York. We were represented there by several of our group that are here today and we heard at that meeting about a purity code. This purity code was sent to each school, and I am quite sure you have read it and understand its principles. I trust that we will be guided by those principles, as we are a member of the N.C.A.A."

An article in Morgan's Silver Anniversary Program in 1953 by Revella Clay said:

"By this time, Eddie's supporters were growing. Dr. Dwight Oliver Wendell Holmes, Dr. John Oakley Spencer, Dr. Charles Campbell (team physician), Professor Theodore R. Stills (history professor and team statistics), Mr. James H. Carter, Mr. Edward N. Wilson (Morgan comptroller), Dean George C. Grant (who had missed only a few games in a quarter of a century), President Martin D. Jenkins, and Maryland Governor Theodore R. McKeldin were Bear supporters and Eddie Hurt fans."

Great as Eddie Hurt was in football and other sports such as basketball, boxing, tennis, and wrestling, it was not likely that the thin coach and mathematics and physical education professor could dream of what was ahead for him as a track coach. Morgan's record in track and field had been phenomenal for two decades. The orange and blue-clad Bears had won or tied approximately 18 CIAA open championships. Morgan trackmen had set 9 of 18 individual CIAA track records compiled between 1922 and 1950.

The world was not ready for this avalanche of heat and speed that Hurt was preparing for the athletic world from a different direction. Hurt and the Morgan Bears became almost an overnight phenomenon. In a few short years, his men had spanned the globe, running and setting records throughout the United States, South America, Europe, the Far East, and ultimately to the Olympic games. Leading into that explosion is a small dissertation on Hurt's ability to handle young men and get the most of their abilities, both emotionally and physically.

Many of Hurt's rivals attributed his success to his proficiency in mathematics, which they claimed enabled him to develop intricate plays based upon precise timing. Some analysts felt that it was the quiet man's uncanny psychology, his manner of handling men and inspiring them to exceed what appeared to be their natural abilities. Reflecting back to 1952 in a game with Howard University, Eddie's star offensive/defensive tackle, Roosevelt Brown, (Hall of Fame, New York Giants, N.F.L.) was being double teamed all over the field. Along about the fourth quarter, Brown was bleeding from the mouth and nose. He had been taking an awesome beating and the game was close. It was a tribute to the fortitude and courage of any man to hang in there so long. During a time-out, "Roosy" (as his teammates referred to him), ran over to the bench, and, at the sight of him, many on the bench got sick, but Roosy grabbed a towel, wiped his face, and looking at Coach, said, "Don't worry Coach. I'm going back in there and push them to the other end of the field." He did just that. Hurt could look at a young man, and with his hands in his pocket (some people said holding up his pants), could curl his lips down or up depending upon the situation, and inevitably change the entire mood of a depressed player ready to throw in the towel. Others were more prone to believe that Eddie's success was his ability to take a young man of reasonable athletic ability, tune his body to a high standard of physical fitness, teach him to obey the exigencies of the game without crying, and by doing so, instill self-discipline and confidence in the athlete. Much of this can be of great educational value, and with the proper scholastic training for mental alertness, can and has provided the substance that made great men of young boys. Many of Eddie's "boys" attest to that fact today.

Co-Captain Roosevelt Brown...Offensive Tackle Morgan State College New York Giants N.F.L., Hall of Fame

Co-Capt - William Buford Tackle opposite Brown

The seed for the track team was planted back in 1946. One of Coach Hurt's athletes, Elmore "Pepper" Harris, was running for an American team touring the Island of Jamaica. "Pepper" was impressed with a young sprinter from Panama by the name of Samuel LaBeach. Sam, a gifted athlete, was interested in obtaining a college education. With "Pepper's" assistance, Sam contacted Coach Hurt and eventually entered Morgan State. Hurt was elated to learn that Sam was from a family of great Jamaican runners. His two brothers, Lloyd and Byron, were also world-class sprinters and future Olympians. Sam was able to convince Byron to attend Morgan but Lloyd went elsewhere. This "Jamaica Connection" proved very productive for Coach Hurt, since LaBeach introduced him to another great sprinter, George Rhoden. Rhoden entered Morgan in 1948 and thus began a truly great period of track and field history. There was one last major piece of the puzzle required. About this time, William "Bill" Brown, returning from the service, entered Morgan State. Bill was destined to become one of America's great half-milers and a world-class quarter-miler. He also ran overseas for his country.

After a few years of a conscientious training program, which emphasized physical fitness and the development of the proper mental approach, Hurt saw that his labor was beginning to bear fruit.

Hurt was one of the first black college coaches to bring national and international fame to a Negro college. Beginning with the 1950 Penn Relays held in Philadelphia's Franklin Field, Morgan has become a big name in track news throughout the world. Hurt's foursome of Sam LaBeach, Bob Tyler, Bill Brown, and George Rhoden won the mile relay in 3:13.6 which broke the Penn Relay's record that had stood for fifty-six years. LaBeach, Tyler, and Brown had built up a short lead of two strides during the first three legs of the race, but the 30,000-plus fans in Franklin Stadium were screaming as the great Reggie Pearman of New York University received the baton on the anchor leg. Reggie was undoubtedly one of the world's best quartermilers, and had never been defeated in the relays. Immediately, he cut the lead to one stride. Anchorman for Morgan was the great quartermiler, Jamaican-born George Rhoden, who had also gained fame by winning the National AAU quartermile championship.

1950 Great Mile Relay Team
Tyler, Rhoden, Brown, LaBeach and Coach Hurt

The two quartermilers matched each other stride for stride down the long backstretch of Franklin Field, which has brought to ruin many aspiring quarter-milers, for as one came off the backstretch, he would run head-on into what has long been described as "rigor mortis corner". Usually at this point, most aspiring quarter-milers prepared to turn on the after burners and come on home on a wing and a prayer. However, what has transpired over the years has been a massive buildup of delirious track fans consisting of fraternities, sororities, and most of the major participating college and university fans, who collect at the third bend and wait to watch "riggie" claim his runners.

The diagnosis for rigor mortis usually begins with the runner suddenly straightening up, his stride cut in half, and his track shoes appearing to turn to concrete. He can no longer get his knees up high, his eyes tend to become fixed and bulge outward, and his entire face becomes a twisted mass of frozen flesh. All of this occurs as he painfully approaches that little white line marking the end of the quartermile where he is, amidst thundering roars of laughter, (sympathetic laughter), permitted to gracefully fall.

But on this day, something different happened. The fans were watching the world's classiest runners perform. Reggie kept his eyes on Rhoden, preparing to take him on rigor mortis corner, but the long-legged Jamaican didn't slow down. The two men reached down deep and kept their legs and arms pumping, taking in greater amounts of oxygen as their lungs were on fire, and every muscle ached. Rhoden heard Eddie Hurt's great exhortation, "Run from there, George!" and he reached down into his innermost being, strained hard, and the two great runners crossed the finish line exactly one stride apart. A few weeks later, Hurt's team received an invitation to run in the Coliseum Relays in Los Angeles, California. The historic four ran 3:9.4 mile relay which was just two seconds off the world record at that time. The foresome returned to a hero's welcome, and they became good will ambassadors for the college both nationally and internationally.

In the CIAA Championships held in May 1950, Morgan won easily. The 440-yard record was broken by Rhoden. His wining time was 47.9. In the 880-yard run, Bill Brown set a record, winning in 1:53.9. Thurlow Brown demonstrated his great capabilities as a distance runner and Lester Scott broke the 110-yard high-hurdle record, winning with a time of 14.6. The Morgan mile relay team broke the CIAA record, winning in 3:12.5. Hurt took his team that year to the following meets: Indoors, they ran in the Washington Evening Star Games, the Philadelphia Inquirer, Seton Hall Relays, South Atlantic Meet, the Melrose Games, the N. Y. Knights of Columbus, Boston Athletic Association, and the National AAU Championships at

Madison Square Garden. Hurt also participated in the following outdoor competitions: Seton Hall Relays, Penn Relays, the National (NCAA) Meet, the National AAU, the South Atlantic Championships, and the California Coliseum Meet. Morgan placed fifth in the NCAA Track and Field Championships at the University of Minnesota. They made 36 points in the Junior National AAU Championships at the University of Maryland. They won nine national championships during the 1950 track season, and also won the freshman mile relay at the Penn Relays. They also won the National AAU Relay Championship, the 1600-meter Relay Championship, and the 400-meter Relay Championship. Considering the size of Morgan College (1600 students) compared to the size of the other NCAA schools, these accomplishments seem on the miraculous side.

It is interesting to note that prior to the 1950s' relay victories at Franklin Field, most of the running by Negro colleges had been the "B" level. Hurt put an end to that procedure as he went on to retire the Penn Relay 4x100 and 4x200 relay championships.

Young black men across the country were beginning to dream of great things. Jackie Robinson broke the color barrier into the major leagues on April 10, 1947. Roosevelt Brown, one of Hurt's boys and a Morgan all-time great, was drafted by the New York Giants and went on to the NFL Hall of Fame. Brown, although not the first to be drafted from a black college, was one of the initial group to be successful.

In basketball, Duquesne University had an excellent star, Charles Cooper. Cooper, from Pittsburgh, Pennsylvania, was drafted into the professional ranks by the Boston Celtics, the first of his race. The Celtics owner, Walter Brown, when told Cooper was a colored boy, responded, "I don't give a damn if he is striped or plaid or polka dot!" (M. Lawrence, The Pittsburgh Press, "Blazing a Trial From the Bluff," April 7, 1991). Obviously, Mr. Brown was far ahead of his peers. The athletic world was undergoing a major transformation. In the span of a few years, the Brooklyn Dodgers, the pride of Ebbot's Field, was playing such black talent as Roy Campanella, Don Newcombe, and Joe

Black, a Morgan man, in addition to Robinson. Many baseball men will tell you Newcombe and Black were two of the very best pitchers in the Majors.

After LaBeach, Tyler, Brown, and Rhoden departed from Morgan in the early 1950s many sport enthusiasts thought that the glory years of track fame were over. It would be extremely difficult to replace Olympic and national champion runners, but by this time, Morgan State had obtained national prominence. In fact, one could travel all over Europe and the Far East and the name Morgan State would cause ears to perk up.

The list of black athletes began to grow like a great swell upon the sea. Granted, there was no room for mediocrity. Only the best of the athletes could make the grade, but the tide had changed.

Eddie Hurt looked at this phenomenon in a slightly philosophical manner. He would often drift back into the '30s and think of "Tank" or "Brutus" and analytically attempt to compare them with the current cream of the crop. He would hunch over in his favorite version of the hit man with his coat turned up and his hands in his pockets and, mumbling to himself, compare his 1933 and 1949 teams with the fighting Irish or the Nittany Lions of Penn State University. Then he would look off into the distance as if he could really see his Bears fighting on the gridiron in a great mythical match of the Four Horsemen face-to-face, Notre Dame and Morgan State, the "Apocalypse." Finally, he would pick up his gait and (you could almost feel the power of his intellect) cry out, "Let's go to work!" It didn't matter whether it was a scrimmage or a time trial; they all ended the same way. Strong young men dripping wet, some half walking, half crawling, some dazed from the intensities of the workout, slowly vanishing toward the showers.

Hurt knew in the early '50s what the forecast was to be. He saw the handwriting on the wall. But as the slow, hardly noticeable recruiting drive by white colleges began, few others foresaw the tremendous deluge of scouts and recruiters descend upon the unsuspecting black colleges. The schools were hit by an avalanche in which nearly all of the great talent which had been hidden for decades was swept up, leaving many black schools nearly destitute of first class talent.

Hurt busied himself in the early '50s, taking advantage of the huge awakening that such events as the Olympics, Penn Relays, the great indoor track meets which criss-crossed the East Coast from Boston to Washington D.C. had brought.

Bill Brown NCAA Half-Mile Champion 1950

Bill Brown, C IAA Half-Mile Champion, 1950

George Rhoden
Olmpic Gold Medal
World Record Holder 45.8

When Art Bragg (NCAA and AAU 100-meter champion) first arrived on Morgan's campus and reported for his first day of track practice as a walk-on, he was slowly pacing off what he felt was 100 meters. (The track field had not yet been marked out.) He heard Coach's scratchy but strong voice call all the runners over to him at the starting line and announce very quietly that he would have time trials that day. Bragg was a rather carefree, unconcerned kid who didn't cause any trouble, nor did he look for any. In fact, he was known to have taken ten minutes just to walk 100 meters. He couldn't understand the need for rushing or even getting excited. His metabolism must have set world records for deceleration while walking, but the most amazing transformation took place in him starting hours prior to a race until at some undiscovered moment, he became, in a split second, the fastest human in the world.

Arthur Bragg
NCAA 100 Meter Champion

Every Morganite and most sports writers who witnessed Art running will verify that statement. But Morgan almost lost him after he ran his first and last quarter-mile time trial. The story has it that he disappeared immediately after picking himself off the ground two feet on the other side of the quarter-mile finish line, not to be seen again for three whole days. Perhaps if Hurt ever lost a battle, it was to Bragg because Bragg just didn't like running quarter-miles. When Hurt saw him later that week and inquired as to his whereabouts, the only thing Bragg said was, "Wah, wah." Hurt put his hands in his pocket, turned around, and quickly walked away, choosing to wait and fight another day.

Bragg's starts were initially terrible. He resembled a gooney bird taking off. So coach and pupil persevered through months of refining his starts, which varied between false starts, slow starts, and no starts at all. But when the right chemistry finally put everything into proper perspective, feet apart, hands apart, hips slightly raised, almost on a level with the ground, Bragg exited the starting blocks as though shot from a cannon.

As the weeks progressed, Bragg demonstrated he was a true sprinter. He had a tendency to slow down after obtaining fantastic speeds between 60 and 90 yards. Hurt saw that Bragg had a tendency to drop his arms and stop acceleration at about the 60-yard mark. He decided that now he would even the score, even though by this time, he and Bragg had become inseparable, coach and pupil, coach and friend. Hurt suggested that at the 60-yard mark, Bragg should take a deep breath and let it out with a loud "Waah!" This indeed improved his acceleration. It became a great phenomenon at Morgan, since all the runners began to end every sentence they spoke with "Waah." As the story goes, it caused great concern since none of the college's professors could agree on whether it was a noun, adjective, or verb.

Art Bragg and Coach Hurt

Bragg went on to become the National AAU 100-yards Champion, National NCAA 100-yards champion, and CIAA champion in 100- and 200-yards for the years 1950-52. He also became a member of the US Olympic track team (Finland), and traveled to such foreign land as New Zealand, England, Scotland, Ireland, Germany, Italy, and Switzerland.

Art Bragg wins the Penn Relay 100 meters

In the 1952 Olympic trials, he won his qualifying heat and was keeping the pressure off his legs by easing up just enough to ensure qualifying. He had previously beaten Lindy Remagino of Manhattan College and was the favorite for a gold medal. While warming up for another trial race, he was accidentally injured. Without sufficient time to recover, he was unable to compete in the Olympic finals. Without sufficient time to recover, he did not run in the Olympic finals. Remagino went on to win the Olympic gold medal. Remagino was a definite world-class sprinter, so no attempt is made here to discredit his fantastic feat of wining the Olympic gold. It is just that the world would have enjoyed watching the two of them head-to-head in the championships.

The United States has its secrets, and so did Morgan State. Morgan had a secret that most other coaches never found out about until it was too late. Hurt had a theory in the early 1950s which was rather simple and to the point. Everyone on Morgan's track team had to run the quarter-mile. Hurt believed that if a man had two strong legs, strong lungs, a big heart, and intestinal fortitude, he could make that man a world-class runner. Although the thought might sound somewhat simplistic, truth is stranger than fiction, and much more interesting. Hurt believed that you could take a young man who had a little talent, place him beside an Olympic or NCAA champion, give him a feel for what it's like to run with real class, and if he sustains that first shock of eating cinders and running through smoke, maybe he would have something with which to work. This psychology worked. Out of the fiery trial came Hurt's second assault upon the collegiate thinclads. These were free running, give-it-all-you've got, all-the-way kind of runners like Bernard Boasmond, Howard Morgan, Byron LaBeach, Clover Street, Louis Goodman, and, six months later, Josh Culbreath, Otis "Jet" Johnson, Robert Robinson, Jim Rogers, Herman "Bitsy" Wade, Charles K. Mills, Eugene Thomas, and Earl Graves. Later on, they included a great freshman class of runners like Lawrence Griffin of Dunbar High School, Herbert Washington of Armstrong High in Washington, D.C., Donald "Jabbo" Johnson of Schenley High school, Pittsburgh, Kenneth Kave, of Dunbar in D.C., Edward Waters of

Douglas High School in Baltimore, and Wardell Stansbury of Harvre-D-Grace, Maryland.

With Bragg heading up his track team, Hurt had little problem attracting some of the best black talent available. His Baltimore and Washington farm system (graduates of Morgan coaching in the public school system) constantly kept him supplied with raw talent. Eddie never addressed his friends as members of his farm system but since the city school system employed many of his former students as teachers and coaches, it was unspecified but accepted that he received first choice.

Very few old-timers can forget that fateful day in the summer of 1953 at the CIAA Track Championships. Bragg, the premier sprinter in the world, was literally run off the track by three hungry local protégés Hurt had recruited from Baltimore and D.C. schools. The event was the CIAA 100-yard dash championship being held at Morgan. Bragg had planned an easy win. He warmed up just enough to get his legs loose and then prepared to run. Lining up with Bragg were three Morgan freshmen who had qualified for the finals: Ken Kave, Dickey Waters, and Lawrence Griffen. At the sound of the starter's pistol, Bragg was out of the blocks like a bolt of lightning. Apparently, he figured he would blow away the freshmen early and discourage them. However, to his and the spectators' dismay, at the 50-yard mark, the freshmen were moving stride for stride with the world's fastest human. Many old-timers who were present will tell you the look on Bragg's face went from peace to panic. He began to frantically pump his arms and drive his powerful legs like pistons, but it was to no avail. The freshmen refused to drop back and continued stride for stride with him. When you think about it, nine seconds is hardly more than a few blinks of the eye, so when Bragg saw the finish line, the old seasoned warrior pulled his last remaining fox-like move. Before the startled freshmen realized what had happened, Bragg leaned his body into the stretched-out tape so far it appeared he had won by a comfortable margin. When the officials checked all the stopwatches, the truth was shocking. All the sprinters had the same time: 9.5 seconds (It doesn't get any closer than that!).

*Art Bragg, Ken Kave, Dickey Waters, and Lawrence Griffen
CIAA 100 meters championship*

Hurt put his second mile relay team together in the spring of 1952. After a series of strenuous workouts and time trials, he decided upon a solid sophomore quartet: Wade, Johnson, Rogers, and Culbreath. This team proceeded to wreak havoc from Boston through Madison Square garden in New York City to the Enquirer games in Philadelphia and the Evening Star Games in Washington, D.C.

The team's runners were smaller than the exceptionally tall 1950 team. Therefore, Hurt would always explain the phenomenon of their indoor success by the shortness of their legs, which he said enabled them to run the fast times on the indoor boards much more smoothly than the taller 1950 quartet. He saw greatness in both teams but for different reasons.

His theory was correct since the sophomores went on to break the National AAU standards in the Gardens and set new collegiate records from Boston to Washington, D.C. However, since records are made to be broken, no conclusions can be drawn from that feat. The flying four, led by their gutsy Olympic star Josh Culbreath, spent all of their time together. They trained as a team, ate together, enjoyed each other's company, and inspired each other to greater achievements. Culbreath and Rogers, the mathematician, and presently an urologist in Philadelphia, would plot their times on a graph. Josh would say to Wade: "Number one. You lead off with a 47 flat, and Jet (Johnson), number two, you plan on a 46.5. Jim, number three, we'll count on you for a 46 flat, and I'll anchor with a 46.5." The team would really run for these times for about a 3:06 mile. Running on crushed cinder rather than the mercurial Olympic standard track of today, a 3:06 was highly respectable and usually a winner in the '50s.

The Flying Four were unique in that they constantly kept tabs on one another. As the story goes, one of the four had a girlfriend on campus. It was okay for him to walk and talk with her around the campus but one day, he decided to pull a fast one and go to a movie alone. When number 1, 3, and 4 missed the wayward one, they panicked and headed for town. Since there was only one movie available, they quietly walked in and when their eyes recovered from the light, there sitting in front of them was number 2 with his arm around his girlfriend. There was so much talk and laughter going on behind him that number 2 sheepishly removed his arm from his date and slowly headed for the campus.

Bobby Gordon
220 yard Dash Champion

*Joshua "Josh" Culbreath
Olympic 400-meter hurdles
Bronze Metal*

*Paul Winder
100/200 meter Champion
Olympian*

The practice of referring to each other in terms of numbers has continued to the present with the Flying Four.

The "Flying Four": Josh Culbreath, Jim Rogers, Otis Johnson, Herman Wade

Hurt, forever the thinking man, always fought the odds with true cunning. He was faced with the challenge of three major opponents which all had Olympic caliber quarter-milers anchoring their mile relays. Manhattan College had Olympian Lou Jones anchoring, the mile relay. University of Pittsburgh had American record holder, and Olympian, Arnie Sowell, and Villanova University had Olympic gold medal winner Charlie Jenkins. Hurt's thinclads, such as Jim Rogers, Otis Johnson, and Josh Culbreath, also an Olympian, were all equally talented. However, Hurt devised another strategy, which proved highly successful. Instead of placing Jim Rogers, CIAA open quarter champion, his fastest quarter-miler, as anchorman, Hurt slipped Rogers to the third leg and let his more experienced Pan American champion, Josh Culbreath, anchor. The effort was devastating to Hurt's opponents because the first three runners would build up a commanding lead, and then Culbreath had plenty of room to keep that pack of super runners behind.

Many thought that Hurt had another purpose in his tactic. He loved to hear the announcer at Madison Square Garden say "Anchoring for Morgan Sate is Josh Culbreath, National AAU 400-meter hurdle champion, Pan American Champion," etc. Hurt would grin his approval, and Culbreath would, at each enumeration of his feats, lift his knees a little higher, like a victorious stallion, and prance across the tape. Josh would take his victory lap blowing kisses to the fans as was the tradition; Hurt obviously felt that all the fanfare might attract a few more aspiring champions to Morgan, and so it did.

Hurt outdid himself, however, when he arranged a match race between the Flying Four and the world-renowned team called the Grant Street Boys of New York City. The Grant Street Boys consisted of four Olympic champions and world record holders. Hurt knew all about the laws of physics, but he apparently had a hypothesis he wanted to test out. As it turned out, his hypothesis was wrong. What he needed was four portable jet engines that he could have attached to the Flying Four; they really needed them. The Grant Street Boys consisted of then graduated George

Rhoden, Gold medallist world record holder for the 400-meter at 45.8; Andy Stanfield, gold medal winner in the 100-200 meter; Herb Mckinley, Olympic gold medal winner; and Mel Whitfield, Olympic gold and world record holder, 800 meters.

The race was set for the Baltimore Armory and that night, the place was filled to capacity. Hurt called his thin clads over and began to explain his hypothesis. Though a little pale and highly nervous, the Flying Four were game. Hurt had rearranged the running sequence, apparently taking advantage of each runner's strength in relation to the Grant Street Boys. At the sound of the starter's gun, Andy Stanfield took off as though he were attempting to match the speed of light. The huge crowd gave a loud yell and that might have been the death cry for the marvelous Flying Four because they never did see the light in that race. As it was, though, at the finish line, there was only a difference of a second or so, but there was little doubt who won. Eddie let his boys know he was proud of them and disappeared from sight. But the Flying Four knew they hadn't flown at all that night. Their little wings were kind of droopy and they had lost a lot of feathers.

Much has been said about Hurt as the no-nonsense, stern disciplinarian, but he also had a rather sophisticated sense of humor. In 1954, he carried his mile relay team to the New York Armory to run in a special race. The lead-off man thought it strange that he was the only man at the starting line. At the sound of the gun, he ran his quarter-mile and saw no one. Jet Johnson, number-two man, said he heard what sounded like running feet, and as he rounded the final turn, he saw about four other teams ahead of him. Number-three man Jim Rogers knew they were out there, so he ran for all he was worth, and was closing in at the end of his quarter-mile when he passed the baton to the anchorman, Josh Culbreath, yelling, "Run, Josh!" Culbreath remembers running his heart out, and as the team neared the tape, using all his experience, leaned as far as he could. Morgan won the race by a nose. The exhausted team collapsed on the floor, frustrated and hurting. Rogers, looking up at Hurt, managed to ask, "Coach, what kind of race was that?" Hurt looked down at his prostrate team and with a laugh, said, "That was the perfect handicap race!"

Bob McMurray
NCAA 400 Meter Champion

In April of 1970, the Baltimore *Evening Sun* carried an article by Doug Brown about an entirely different side of Hurt. Brown wrote that Morgan was playing a major football game once in which an official was doing a poor job. Coaches submitted written reports, rating the officials on a 100-point system. Hurt, becoming increasingly irritated, decided to give the bad official an earful of what he would put in the report the following Monday. "Intestinal fortitude minus 40!" Hurt shouted as the lineman passed the bench. That cost Morgan 15 yards. Two more jibes were good for two more 15-yard penalties. Hurt relented, satisfied that he had made his point, though at a considerable price. Brown also wrote that Morgan used to have a big End who was always making mistakes, jumping off sides, and dropping passes. Before a big game with Howard University in Washington, D.C., old Griffith Stadium, Marse Hill said to the boy, with exasperation in his voice: "Listen, if you make a mistake today, don't wait to be told, come out of the game yourself." Morgan had the ball on Howard's 15-yard line, fourth down, behind by one touchdown. The quarterback called a pass, the big miscreant ran a dandy pattern, got wide open, and then dropped the perfect pass. The ball changed hands and Morgan went on defense. (There was no platooning in those days.) After Howard had run a few plays, it dawned on Hurt and Hill that they were playing with only ten men. Hurt looked down the bench and there at the end of the bench, all alone, was the big End. As instructed, he hadn't waited to be told to come out after making a mistake. Brown wrote, "Eddie Hurt, Morgan State's 143-pound track coach, 66 years old then, crouched in the starting blocks. Words had failed, so Hurt was going to show this kid how to bolt from the blocks. 'I beat him, too' Hurt recalls. Forty yards it was. I also pulled a muscle although I tried not to show it.' That was Eddie Hurt."

Bob Barksdale - High Jump Champion
NY Athletic Club 1956

John Bethea
CIAA Hurdles Champion

George Dennis
High Jump Champion
(Picture Not Shown)

Morgan State College Track Teams

1941 Track Team

1947 Track Team

1948 Track Team

1949 Track Team

1955 CIAA Track and Field Champions

1957 CIAA Track and Field Champions

More of Hurt's Track and Field Greats

William Byron

William "Sugar" Cain

Bill Brent

John Tripplet

Nick Ellis
CIAA 440yd Champion

Lee Martin

Herbert Washington

Roland Brown

Bobbie Robinson

Thomas Tipton

Don Johnson

B. Mills

W. Stansbury

McKinley Crews

Earl Graves

Morgan State College Football Teams

1940 CIAA Champions

1933 UNDEAFTED team

1949 Football Team

1953 Football Team Pep Talk for Coaches Boys

1953 Football Team

Row 1: W. Robbins, C. Whitted, E. Covert, W. Buford, M. Marcus, J. Locust, R. Brown, E. Lindsay, P. Graham, T. Holly, G. Williams, R. Morton. **Row 2:** K. Brown (Asst. Line Coach), E. P. Hurt (Head Coach), J. White, P. Smith, L. Harrell, H. Hughes, J. Scott, D. Patterson, G. Freeman, W. Bishop, J. Green, W. Carr, O. Johnson, W. Mosley, T. L. Hill (Head Line Coach), A. Brown (Asst. Backfield Coach). **Row 3:** J. Stevenson, S. Gumbs, J. Austin, J. Gamble, J. Cassidy, J. Davis, T. Murray, R. Cropper, C. Gibson, G. McKinney, A. Scott. **Row 4:** G. Martin, E. Williams, T. Dorsey, G. Prather, J. Bostic, A. Gaines, L. Randall, D. Perguson, D. Chapman. R. Colbert, E. O'Kelley, J. Ware, E. Hunter, A. Jefferson.

1955 Football Team

More of Hurt's Football Greats

Locust

Tim Howard

Marcus

Roy Cragway

Joe Black of Brooklyn Dodger Fame

Clarence "Big House" Gaines
Winston Salem Athletic Director

Mel Hurt
Col. US Army

Alvin "Boo" Brown
Morgan Coach
Medical Doctor/Educator

Len Ford
Cleveland Browns

George Rooks

Tippy Day

Eugene Lonney

Quarterback, Gary Freeman

Morgan State College 1953 Boxing Team

K. Brown (Coach), Eubanks, Williams, White, Dismond, Mello, Lindsay (Trainer), Barron (Manager).

Morgan State College 1953 Wrestling Team

Pumphrey, Wilson, Morton, Harrell, Brown, Graham, Jubilee, Williams, Hemming

Morgan State College Swimming Team

1953 Swim Team

1955 CIAA Swimming and Diving Champions

Row 1: W. Wilson (Mgr), K. Graham (Co-Capt.), S. Brooks (Coach), C. Cooper (Co-Capt.). **Row 2:** R. Kelly, J. Newton, L. Montgomery, D. Dixon, S. Gumbs, W. Dalton, G. Douglass, L. Young, D. Garlington, C. Brown, A. Jenkins, J. Williams.

Morgan State College Basketball Team

1931 CIAA Champions

Some of Hill's Basketball Greats

**Co-Captains 1954
left: Bob Thweatt
right: George Williams**

1955 Basketball Team Members
Morgan State University Yearbook 1955

CHAPTER IV

HONORS

One evening while sitting talking to Coach Hurt about his life, the subject of honors came up. Coach looked up as if he were staring into space and said, "I've had all the honors I need." I was not certain I understood, so I attempted to explore the subject in greater depth. But he wouldn't elaborate on his statement. About that time, the telephone rang, and Mom Hurt informed her husband that it was for him. He picked up the phone and said, "Hello?" I noticed a great change in his voice then, and much excitement covered his face. He said to me, "It's Art Bragg! He's calling me from California." As I listened to the conversation, the answer came to me: Ed Hurt didn't find his rewards in trophies or banquets but in the fruits of his labor – his boys. His interest in athletes didn't stop the day they graduated from college; he kept them in his heart always. Their interests, problems, and successes were the real trophies, the real honors. When he finished talking on the telephone, he looked renewed, and so did Mom Hurt.

"Mom" Hurt

Sign of the Times for Football Mentors

The phenomenon continued all through the time I was privileged to visit their lovely home. First LaBeach would call, then Culbreath, Jim Rogers, Otis Trump, Red Roberts, "Jet" Johnson and the list goes on.

I cannot dismiss the "official" honors, though, because Hurt had by his works carved out quite a tall mountain of mementos, artifacts, awards, honors, and countless intangible achievements which may never be measured or quantified.

He was a small man in stature, so one doesn't think of him as a person who kicked down doors. Perhaps, though, that's exactly the way to think of him. A small man who is dedicated to his work, determined, and intelligent, actually opens doors. Hurt's convictions helped to change society. It was too bad Halley's comet didn't brighten the heavens on his birth date, for the coming of Eddie Hurt was an event.

In 1949, Eddie received a note from the Honorable Armond W. Scott, and James G. Tyson, Toastmaster of the Washington Pig Skin Club, to attend their banquet. He was totally surprised and insisted that Marse Hill attend with him. Sitting at the head table that night were Branch Rickey, President of the Brooklyn Dodgers; Marion Motley, all-pro fullback (1948) of the Cleveland Browns; Bob Morganito, Head Coach of Georgetown University's football team; Honorable William L. Dawson, Congressman from Illinois; Howard T. Bailey, Director of Washington Evening Star Games; and Mark Cardwell, Coach of West Virginia State College. Hurt was named Coach of the Year by the Club. He took the award in his characteristic modest and sober manner. However, as he and Marse Hill reflected on it days later, they felt as though they were the antipathy of the Dodgers' Branch Rickey: they saw him kicking down the door from one side while they assaulted it from the other side.

Such parallelism was the dawning of a great reformation in America's sports world. Here was Rickey, a great man who had the intelligence, foresight, and intestinal fortitude to open up America's favorite pastime, baseball, to its black population. Now every American boy could aspire to the wonderful dream of being a baseball star. Rickey did not know that the small man from Morgan had been preparing one of his future stars, a young, hard throwing pitcher named Joe Black, to become an instant star on his beloved team.

Rickey could not have known that Hurt was destined for greatness in his own right. But again, perhaps it was the times that Rickey was destined to be great by having convictions, and, believing in them, was prepared to stand up and be counted amidst great opposition. By doing so, he endeared himself in the hearts of men by letting his convictions change society. And the small dark man sitting at the same table with him, a man living and working in the same universe on a parallel line which was black (separate but equal), was literally made of that same unfathomable ingredient which constitutes greatness. We are told by the world's top theoretical scientists that parallel lines could possibly meet, and today, looking at the professional sports of this country, who could doubt it?

The following year, 1950, Hurt received notification from the University of Texas of his selection as one of the outstanding football coaches of all times. This was a singular honor that he and Hill were ecstatic about. They had not realized that they had made an impact so deep into the Southwest.

These kinds of honors only seemed to drive Eddie to tackle more difficult tasks. He became a kind of perpetual motion machine. As Athletic Director, he began to seek tougher opponents and where he could, he opened a new door. He finally began to understand what some of his contributions really meant. Essentially, they had to do with the status and quality of the American sports of football, basketball, track, and baseball in our black colleges. Hurt never saw his honors as personal but rather looked upon them as a reasonable extension of the quality of the black athlete.

The years of hard drills and execution of intricate plays were paying off. His boys could make the transition to professional-level sports and understand the language. The many years of attendance at football and basketball seminars taught by the foremost sports personalities were now beginning to pay dividends. But it did not stop at Morgan College because the entire CIAA was following Hurt's lead, and other schools were also producing quality, well-trained black athletes.

Seldom will you find a coach who in the space of a few years can point to such great acclaim. In 1950, *Track and Field News* named Hurt Track and Field Coach of the Year, an honor recognizing the fantastic season his Olympic and NCAA thinclads had. Much has already been noted concerning 1950. However, it had been in the cinder path world that Hurt won the most widespread acclaim. It was he who gained the respect for the small black college when he dared to put Morgan's one-mile relay team against the nation's best at the Penn Relays. There, Sam LaBeach, Bob Tyler, Bill Brown, and George Rhoden ran a 3:13.6 mile to win. From that moment on, Morgan became a power and a name that required respect wherever Hurt took his team. During 1950, his team had fantastic success running in the following meets: The Washington Evening Star; the Philadelphia Inquirer, Seton Hall Relays, South Atlantic meet; the Melrose Games; the Knights of Columbus and the National AAU Championships at Madison Square Garden. Outdoors, Hurt entered his team in the Seton Hall Relays; Penn Relays; National AAU Meet; and NCAA Championships. Morgan's student population was only 1,600 at the time.

Honors continued to pour in during the 1950s. Morgan State's Student Council presented Hurt with a scroll for unusual achievement. It seems the student body was enjoying the school's unprecedented popularity.

In 1952, the event that probably had the most lasting emotional effect on Hurt occurred. The newly constructed gymnasium was named the Edward P. Hurt Gymnasium by the State of Maryland and Morgan College. It is seldom that one is honored by his peers in his own backyard, and especially when the individual is still alive to smell the roses. But Eddie had gained so much support and popularity that it was done. This writer was present that day and recalls Coach Hurt being visibly shaken and perhaps slightly confused. He had a favorite statement back then, "Heaven is my home, Herman, but I ain't homesick." The honor was so awesome that somehow I felt Hurt thought they should have waited until he went home. But there was something very special about giving him roses while he could still enjoy them. What would have happened to Hurt if he could have seen the awards to come? For example, he received the Baltimore Urban League's Distinguished Service Award in 1953, an award unparalleled in its implications of a person's contribution to his race.

Edward P. Hurt Gymnasium
Campus of Morgan State University

The installation of Hurt into the Helms Foundation Hall of Fame in 1953 was another first for a coach of a primarily black college. The Helms Foundation award probably surprised Eddie, but again, his accomplishment as described in earlier chapter, was unchallengeable. The Morgan State College Alumni Award was presented to him in 1954, followed by Howard University's Department of Physical Education Achievement Award in 1958, and the Morgan State Varsity "M" Club Award in 1959. Hurt had always had a close affinity for Howard University, extending back to his own days there.

After Bea, the Omega Psi Phi Fraternity was Hurt's heart. Thinking back to those latter years in the '80s, the author remembers the joy of being with Hurt as he sang and recited poetry. He knew every fraternity and sorority song on Morgan's campus, and once the two of us had completed a few off-key melodies, Coach would start reciting poetry. His favorite game was to recite a poem and then wait for me to render one. Usually after a few rounds of this, I would shift over to some favorite biblical passage in order to keep up, and Coach would graciously accept my efforts with approval. His dog, a large German Shepherd named Omega, was his constant companion. He was Hurt's protector. On numerous occasions, the author almost lost a toe or heel by making a friendly gesture toward Coach, unfortunately misinterpreted by Omega.

Omega Psi Phi Fraternity presented Eddie its Builder of Character and Champions Award in 1959. This award from his beloved fraternity occupied that special place in his heart, which made him extremely proud.

Up to this point, the awards and honors were either for track accomplishments or for overall achievement in the field of coaching. But in 1959, members of the Coaches Association of America and the United Press honored Hurt by listing him among football coaches for the year 1959. He was the first black coach mentioned in this manner, and the honor came as a welcome surprise to him. The author asked Coach about this honor in relation to other great black coaches in the CIAA and other black conferences. Coach mentioned two others: Mark Cardwell of West Virginia (Yellow Jackets) and Ed Robinson of Grambling College. Mark Cardwell's Yellow Jackets beat Hurt 20-0 in 1945. Hurt came back in 1946 with a 14-13 victory. In 1950 at the National Classic, the teams tied 6-6. Hurt called Mark Cardwell one of the best. Earlier, it was pointed out that Cardwell was a guest at the 1949 Washington Pigskin Club Banquet. Coach Hurt also recalled his clashes with Grambling in the 1940s. In many cases during those early years, Hurt taught Coach Robinson a lesson. But he reminded me that Robinson was a great coach. Robinson started coaching at Grambling around 1941. By that time, the Hurt/Hill combination had an almost fourteen-year head start. Hurt had learned to take life as he encountered it. He had many great stars; men who would have been outstanding in the National Football League. Hurt named a few: Elmore "Pepper" Harris, Brutus Wilson, Otis Troupe, Alvin Brown, Clarence "Big House" Gaines, Joe Black, Mel Hurt, Oscar Given, William Cain, Kenneth Brown, Terry Day, Roy Cragway, Russell Young, Theron Banks, Thomas Hasty, Tillman "Tex" Henderson, Irvin Locust, Matthew Marcus, George Rooks, and William Buford. These men are just a few of the athletes who arrived at Morgan a few years too early. Hurt thought Coach Robinson had fantastic successes and hoped he would continue to develop some of the country's best athletes.

In 1959, Hurt was made a member of the United States coaching staff for the Pan American Games. From this point in his career, his national and international acclaim was established.

One problem that continued to bother Hurt was that there was a tremendous outpouring of black talent into the national and international track and field scene and little or no representation on the national AAU or Olympic Committees. As a result, he spoke to his friend Bob Giegenack of Yale University concerning the matter. He learned that to get on the Olympic Committee, certain recommendations were necessary, and more specifically, it was at that time an "insider" type of relationship that was necessary. But Hurt's tremendous successes and honors had placed him in an excellent position to seek confirmation. He never stood back when duty called, and he was a man of impeccable character and moral courage. So he actively sought appointment to the Olympic Committee and with his record and keen judgment concerning the broad area of athletics, he persevered until selected to the Olympic Committee in 1960.

Between the years 1960 and 1964, Hurt concentrated on his status as a member, making contributions and working tirelessly toward achieving the goals of the Olympic Committee. He met the ever-popular and powerful Avery Brundage, Chairman of the Olympic Committee, and with his straightforward and unassuming manner together with his steel-trap mind, he gained respect from all the Committee personnel, both nationally and internationally.

When Bob Giegenack of Yale, one of America's most respected coaches, was selected in 1964 as the head coach of the Summer Olympics in Japan, he nominated Hurt as his Olympic Track and Field Coach. Hurt remembered Bob telling him he was to take responsibility for the men's sprints and relays and field events such as the high jump, broad jump, pole vault, hurdles, relays, etc. Hurt's initial response was "Impossible!" But Bob's confidence in Hurt was unshakable, so Hurt tackled the task with vigor. Naturally, one of his major thrusts outside of the individual events was the relays. One of Hurt's major problems was adhering to the Olympic rules concerning coaches, who were not permitted on the field. Hurt was worried that one or more of his relay men would run outside of the baton-passing lane and thereby get disqualified. Many weeks had gone into preparation and practice, and Hurt ended up sitting in the stands.

Running for the USA in 1964 was "Bullet" Bob Hayes, the world's fastest human. Hurt recalled how, entering into the final leg of the 4x100 relay, the US was a few meters behind the USSR. Hurt could see Hayes getting anxious, and he kept saying to himself, "Wait, Bob! Wait, Bob!" Hayes sprang from his half-crouched position as though shot from a cannon. Eddie remembered sinking into his seat, petrified by the possibility of Hayes being disqualified. But as it happened, the third-leg man made a frantic lunge for Hayes, and the baton changed hands at the last split second. Then it was up to Hayes. Hurt claimed that Hayes ran the 110 meters in world-record time, blowing away the Russian competitor as though he were standing still. Hurt was elated, but right at the tape, Hayes threw the baton into the air as high as he could, and Hurt almost left the planet, thinking his team would certainly be disqualified. Hayes, however, had successfully broken the tape, prior to tossing the baton into the air. Hurt remembered that moment as one of the most hair-raising in his life. His accomplishments as coach of the 1964 Olympic team were outstanding. All of his charges performed far above expectation

Robert Hayes	100m dash	1st – 9.9 (a)
Mel Pender	100m dash	7th – 10.4
Henry Carr	200m dash	1st – 20.3
Paul Drayton	200m dash	2nd – 20.5
Ulis Williams	400m run	5th -
Hayes Jones	100m hurdles	1st – 13.6
Robert Hayes	400m relay	1st – 39.0 (b)
John Thomas	High jump	- 7'1-1/4"
John Rambo	High jump	3rd – 7'1"
Ira Davis	H, S & J	5th – 52'1-1/4"

a = Olympic and World record   b = Ties Olympic and World record.

Bob Giegenack said Hurt was one of the finest coaches and educators he had the pleasure of knowing, and was one of his closest friends. He was a very valuable member of the 1964 coaching staff, tireless, dedicated, and extremely competent. "I smile every time I remember one incident," he said, "We were at an exhibition basketball game between the U.S. and Canada. It was in a small gym, and we were close to the court. As spectators will, I was remarking freely on the plays, good or bad, to my friends. I turned to speak to Lucie (wife) and just at that moment, there was a shout from the crowd. Turning to Eddie, who had been sitting beside me patiently listening to my observations, I asked, 'What happened?' With a twinkle in his eye, Eddie replied, "Coach, if you are going to coach, you have to watch.'"

Hurt received an Olympic Committee Award for Service in 1964. His dedication to the principles of the Olympics and contributions to furthering its goals of athletics among nations will stand as a beacon for those to follow. He continued to serve on the US Olympic Track and Field Committee until 1972.

Hurt was still not finished with his track accomplishments. He went on to develop such great talents as Bob Barksdale, high jumper; James Roland Brown, distance man; McKinley crews, distance man; George Dennis, high jumper; Nicholson Ellis, sprinter; Bobby Gordon, sprinter; Cecil Harris, Gerald Harrison, Linwood Morton, and Bob McMurray. Obviously, there were too many names to mention, but Hurt developed world-class athletes in football, basketball, and track as well.

An interesting event occurred in 1961, which was a singular honor and is worth mentioning. Hurt was named Referee of the 67th Annual Penn Relay Carnival at Franklin Field on April 28-29, 1961. He was the first black referee in the history of the relays, the nation's foremost track and field carnival. This was a truly fitting honor to a man who had just twenty years previously walked a very tight line, using inordinate diplomacy and fighting when necessary to see that his boys could compete on an even basis with the major universities of the country at the Penn Relays. As usual, Hurt took this honor in stride. The soft-spoken man reflected back to the days when his teams were forced to run in the "B" class races. His philosophy of hard work, determination, and perseverance proved to be the answer, and "run from there" paid off not only for his boys but also for himself.

Perhaps if this book succeeds in nothing more than to demonstrate how Hurt accomplished seemingly impossible tasks, and demonstrates his methods in overcoming prejudice and ignorance, it will have achieved its goals. For then, those who read it and perhaps emulate his creeds will possibly in this present day climb even higher mountains.

Hurt continued coaching track and field on an international basis by coaching the US athletes in dual meets against Russian athletes in Kiev, and in other meets in the US.

When Hurt was preparing the US track team for the 1965 dual meet against the Russian team in Kiev, he had taken a portion of the team by plane for a practice meet against a Canadian team. On the return trip, a storm arose and the turbulence was so terrifying, Hurt knew the team was going to be lost. He prayed hard that night. All he could think of were the headlines: "US Track Team Lost In Storm.

Hurt was a man who believed in getting the job accomplished, and on time. He thought some of the recent Olympic mishaps, such as athletes reporting late for events and the confusion which resulted was tragic, but he would not speculate on whose fault they are. He believed that a coach has to foresee such eventualities and act accordingly.

On March 10, 1962, Jesse Abramson, perhaps the nation's foremost track and field writer, paid high tribute to Hurt. The *Herald-Tribune* extended a "Welcome to Uncle Eddie":

"If you see four runners in shorts which seem to spell out Morgan State handling the baton in the ICAAAA mile relay – and you probably will – don't mistrust your eyes.

It will be Morgan State, and the runners are in the ICAAAA because they belong there.

At its last convention, the Intercollegiate Association of Amateur Athletes of America admitted Morgan State to the Lodge, Member No. 66 in the family of the oldest college track and field organization in the United States.

Obviously, the application of the Baltimore co-ed institution, which has a male enrollment of fewer than 1,300, met all the rigid requirements of the old ICAAAA.

We like to think, though, that it was a tribute to Morgan State's track coach, Edward Paulette Hurt, that The Bears of Baltimore are now full-fledged members of the ICAAAA. Otherwise things won't change much for Uncle Eddie and his Morgan State pupils who have been on the scene, local, Eastern, national, and international, for quite a spell, and always seem to be winning the mile relay or making a great run for it in the invitation meets, National AAU indoor championships, the Queens-Iona Relays, the Penn Relays or wherever.

We press box observers think we have discovered a certain style of running. When we see all four members of the mile relay explode off their marks and run like hell as far and as fast as they can, we poke each other in the rib (The Gentleman from the Times uses his pencil), and say 'Runs like a Hurt man.'

Uncle Eddie would be the last man to claim credit for any innovations in running styles or techniques, but the point is that he is recognized by his peers as quite a coaching fella. You'd never hear it from Ed Hurt anyway. He is as soft-spoken and self-effacing as they come. But he believes in hard work and his pupils believe in Hurt, and the combination produces champions and great competitors.

At Morgan State, Hurt became a legend. From 1929 until he retired on doctor's orders to slow down, his football teams won 14 Central Intercollegiate A.A. titles, had 11 undefeated seasons, six of them undefeated and untied, went 54 games in a defeatless string from 1932 to 1938, went through a war season of five games without yielding a point and concluded the Hurt regime with 176 victories, 51 defeats and 18 ties.

Owing to wider exposure and more open competition on a wider scale, Hurt is better known as a track coach, and is devoting himself exclusively to this sport now. At Morgan State, his Bears were perennial kings of the CIAA, and since 1944 have won 10 Penn Relays titles, a dozen National AAU individual titles and, in the last dozen years, six National AAU mile relay titles in Madison Square Garden, and nine NCAA individual titles.

Uncle Eddie had an Olympic winner and world record holder in George Rhoden, the 400-meter winner in the 1952 Helsinki Games. Rhoden was also his anchorman on his first National AAU mile relay championship team, which set an AAU record of 3:19.9. Succeeding teams won in 1954 in a meet-record 3:18.2, in 1955 in 3:18.5, in 1959 in a meet-record 3:16.6, in 1961 a meet-record 3:16.3 and again last week in 3:18.2. His teams have posted four of the five fastest times in the history of the indoor Nationals.

Names of Hurt pupils who have achieved track renown come easily to mind – Rhoden, Elmore Harris, in the 440 and 600, national sprint champions Art Bragg, Bobby Gordon and Paul Winder, half-miler Bill Brown, Bob McMurray and Nick Ellis, high jumpers George Dennis and Bob Barksdale, Olympic medallist Josh Culbreath in the 400-meter hurdles, among others.

Mostly, Morgan State is best known for its mile relay foursomes, and that could be the vehicle for Morgan State's first ICAAAA title in its ICAAAA debut. He'll get no help, though, from the long-time associates he joins in the ICAAAA coaching fraternity."

(Jesse Abramson, "The ICAAAA Welcomes Uncle Eddie," *New York Herald Tribune*, March 10, 1962).

Hurt was honored again in 1975 by the National Track and Field Hall of Fame in Charleston, West Virginia. Inducted along with Hurt were legendary track stars Jim Thorpe, Bill Toomey, Bob Richards, Bobby Morrow, Ralph Metecalfe, and Stella Walsh. Other track greats already inducted included Ralph Boston, Avery Brundage, Babe Dirkson, Jesse Ownes, Cornelius Warmerdam, Bob Mathias, Parr O'Brien, Lee Calhoun, Glenn Cunningham, and Wilma Rudolph. Obviously, the names represent many of the greatest names in trackdom.

The honors continued to mount; however, most of them are listed at the front of the book. In 1970, Hurt received the Governor's Award for 40 years of service to the State of Maryland. He served on the Mayor's Committee on Education and Aging in Baltimore City. He also served the League for Crippled Children, and actively participated on the Appeal Board of Baltimore City's Department of Recreation and the Board of Directors for the Maryland Arthritis Foundation.

Hurt continued to support organizations such as the Urban League and supported and was honored by the NAACP. He maintained a life long relationship with Baltimore sports writer Sam Lacy, who chronicled much of his accomplishments.

In February of 1987, Morgan's athletic department found itself in financial difficulty. Being a state-supported school, much of its success depends upon the amount of funding provided by the state legislature. Going to bat for Morgan and perhaps more specifically for Coach Hurt were two of his top athletes, Josh Culbreath and Joe Black. The two of them addressed their friend, nationally known celebrity/benefactor Dr. Bill Cosby, who held a benefit for Morgan State. He raised a quarter of a million dollars for the athletic program. The author believes that this main impetus was to assist his friends and to meet the people he had long admired – Coach Hurt and his wife, Bea.

CLOSING

In 1953, during the 25th Silver Anniversary, in an article by Revella L. Clay, Hurt was quoted as saying, "In my opinion, we still have not reached the top. We are still trying to climb. If there is anything I can do to help Morgan accomplish this, I'll just hang around and help. No matter what you're doing, you have to dream. You set goals and you try to reach them. I haven't done nearly all I've wanted to do or dreamed of doing in the area of intercollegiate athletics." Despite all the accolades, Hurt maintained that he was no genius, no miracle man; he couldn't pull rabbits out of a hat. "If I have done anything at all, it's been because of the other coaches, the men, the college, the administration, alumni, friends, and just everybody. I've only had one formula, and that's hard work."

It was 35 years ago that Hurt spoke the above words. The author feels he cannot close this chapter in a more befitting way than to paraphrase Hurt's closest friend and associate, Coach Talmadge Marse Hill: Hurt raised "Fair Morgan" from total obscurity to international prominence. He was the atom of dynamic source, which sent the "Bounding Bears" on their many victorious stampedes. He was at all times the master of tact and strategy. He ignited in the soul of every loyal son and daughter that spark of spirit that says I can, I must, and I will succeed. So goes Edward P. Hurt. God bless him and all his loved ones.

Edward Hurt went home to his Heavenly Father on March 24, 1989. He never read this book but loved its title. He is survived by his wife, Bea; his brother, John J. Hurt; sisters Ellie Williams, Appye Bell, and Mabel Hancock; niece Wilhelmina (Billy) and her husband Roy Cragway; godsons, Edward Reid and Williams Jones; and a host of other nieces, nephews, one sister-in-law and many other relatives and friends, throughout this country and aboard.

Major Walter r. Brown, Dean of Men at Hampton Institute, gave the welcome address at Hampton to the CIAA Conferees in 1932:

"A great deal of improvement has been done in the last five years. In the case of officials, we can now take their decisions, and more and more colored men can be trusted to officiate without the teams having a feeling of being unfairly treated. There was a time when only white officials were trusted to be fair, and one occasion I remember in Georgia, there were two officials at one game. One was to officiate during the first half and the other during the second half.

In the matter of our cartoons we are also improving. ***There was a time when a colored man was pictured running down the field with a watermelon in his hands.*** Now the leading papers are glad to have our cartoons."

Eddie Hurt has brought us a long way. I am certain his last words concerning the above statement would be...

"Run From There"

NOTE: The author is certain some immortal Bears' names are missing. After exhaustive searches for missing records, he regrets any omission and humbly requests that they accept his apology. Perhaps they may be found in the bear.

Appeared in the Afro-American (date unknown)

Football Players

1930 Football Team

1930 Scores

Morgan	Opponent	Scores
46	Cheyney	0
20	St. Paul	7
18	A&T	6
0	Union	13
26	Lincoln	6
39	Shaw	0
18	Seminary	0
18	NC State	7
18	Hampton	6

Bell, Alfred
Berry, Deloss
Black, William
Conrad, Thomas
Cottman, Alphonso
Frazier, John
Garretson, George
Goode, Harry
Hicks, Raymond
Hill, Herbert
Hurt, John
Johnson, Alva

1931 Football team

Bell, Alfred
Black William
Chambers, Raymond
Conrad, Thomas
Garretson, George
Gibbs, James
Gibson, Charles
Gibson, Charles
Goode, Harry
Hardy, Earnest

Hill, Herbert
Hurt, John J.
Johnson, Alva
Johnson, Alva
Johnson, Andrew
Kiah, Lycurgus
Kiah, Waldo
Kiah, William
Lewis, William
McDaniels, Nathaniel

Morris, Arnold
Oliver, Isaiah
Parker, Earl
Poag, Thomas
Quillen, Calvin
Taylor, Paul
Whittington, James
Williams, James
Wilson, Howard

1931 Scores

Morgan	Opponent	Scores
12	A&T	0
25	VA Seminary	0
0	Lincoln	12
19	Howard	8
26	NC State	12
0	Hampton	26

1932 Football Team

1932 Scores

Morgan	Opponent	Scores
38	Cheyney	0
33	A&T	0
24	Union	0
29	Lincoln	0
6	Hampton	6
13	Howard	6
33	NC State	0
10	VA State	7

Burkett, Robert M.
Burns, Charles T.
Chaney, Reginald T.
Conrad, Thomas R.
Cottman, Alphonso
Crake, Carl E.
Crawford, Hubert E.
Daye, Cornelle V.
Easton, Douglass B.
Galloway, Lloyd E.
Gibbs, James R.

Hill, Herbert W.
Lewis, William C.
Rosedom, George H.
Ruddock, Newell E.
Sturgis, John I.
Taylor, Paul W.
Thompson, Olin T.
Troupe, Otis E.
Williams, James H.
Williams, Wendell
Wilson, Howard K.

1933 Football Team

Burkett, Robert
Hill, HerbertConrad, Thomas
Holt, Thomas
Taylor, Paul
Crawford, Hubert
Jewett, Hamilton
Thompson, Olin
Drake, Carl
Jordan, Wilbur
Troupe, Otis
Galloway, Lloyd
Lewis, William
William, Edward
Gardner, William
Mack, Chesley
Williams, James
Gibbs, James
Mosby, Walter
Wilson, Howard
Gibson, Charles
Rosedom, George
Woolridge, Thomas
Harmon, Frank
Simpson, William

1933 Scores

Morgan	Opponent	Scores
37	A&T	0
25	Union	0
45	Lincoln	0
60	Bluefield	0
27	Howard	0
47	NC State	0
13	Hampton	6
40	VA State	0

1934 Football Team

1934 Scores

Morgan	Opponent	Scores
7	A&T	0
0	Union	0
19	Lincoln	0
0	Bluefield	0
0	Howard	0
28	Hampton	0
8	VA State	0

Brisco, Ben
Brown, Thomas
Burkett, Robert
Calhoun, John
Campbell, Preston
Chaney, Reginald
Crawford, Hubert
Crake, Carl
Gardner, William
Gibbs, James
Harmon, Frank
Hawkins, Benjamin
Jordan, Theodore
Jordan, Wilbur
Lampkins, William
Lansdowne, Henry
Lewis, William
Mack, Chesley
Phillips, Jesse
Roberts, Richard
Rosedom, George
Simpson, William
Sowell, Richard
Sturgis, John
Troupe, Otis

1935 Football Team

Anderson, Leonard
Crawford Hubert
Maiden, Clarence
Blanks, George
Davis, Wilbert
Mosby, Walter
Bolden, Earl
Gordon, Frank
Owens, Franklin
Brown, Thomas Grant, George
Roberts, Richard
Burkett, Robert
Hardin, Herbert
Ryans, Maso

Calhoun, Jack
Hawkins, Benjamin
Simpson, William
Campbell, Preston
Hurt, Jesse
Sowell, Richard
Chaney, Thomas
Jordon, James
Troupe, Otis
Cheathan, John
Lampkins, William
Webster, James
Crake, Carl
Mack, Chesley

1935 Scores

Morgan	Opponent	Scores
19	A&T	7
13	Union	0
26	Lincoln	0
12	Bluefield	9
39	Howard	0
13	Hampton	0
32	VA State	7

1936 Football Team

Anderson, Leonard
Lane, John
Brown, Thomas
Lewis, Archibald
Campbell, Preston
Maiden, Clarence
Chaney, Richard
Mallory, Charles
Cheatham, John
Mosby, Walter
Cromwell, Horace
Owens, Franklin
Gwathney, James

Roberts, Richard
Hardin, Herbert
Robinson, Walter
Hawkins, Benjamin
Ryans, Maso
Holly, Wayman
Simpson, William
Howard, William
Smith, James
Kee, James
Sowell, Richard
Lampkins, William
Waller, Francis

1936 Scores

Morgan	Opponent	Scores
6	Union	0
13	Lincoln	0
6	Bluefield	6
40	Howard	0
7	Hampton	6
20	A&T	3
6	VA State	6

1937 Football Team

Bowie, Embra
Holley, Wayman
Roberts, Richard
Brandon, Elisha
Hunt, Leon
Robinson, Walter
Bundy, William
Hurt, Jesse
Ryans, Maso
Cain, William
Kee, Horace
Smith, Reuben
Cheathan, John
Kee, James
Smith, Robert
Davis, Wilbur
Lampkins, William

Sowell, Richard
Gibson, Lionel
Maiden, Clarence
Thomas, James
Gordon, Frank
Mosby, Walter
Ruck, Fred
Hampton, Pierce
Nicholas, Lloyd
Tucker, Maurice
Hawkins, Benjamin
Owens, Frank
Waller, Christo
Hill, Laurence
Patterson, Bennie
Watkins, Norman

1937 Scores

Morgan	Opponent	Scores
12	Union	7
19	Lincoln	6
31	Bluefield	0
39	A&T	0
26	Hampton	0
21	VA State	6

1938 Football Team

Bowie, Embra
Kiah, Randolph
Brown, Kenneth
Lewis, Robert
Campbell, Preston
Lindsay, Robert
Cheatham, John
Maiden, Clarence
Gibson, Lionel
Mallory, Ober
Gordon, Frank
Mosby, Wallace
Hampton, Pierce

Nickens, J. Laws
Henderson, Robert
Patterson, Bennie
Hill, Lawrence
Ryans, Maso
Holley, Wayman
Smith, Reuben
Holt, Robert
Smith, Robert
Hunt, Leon
Tucker, Maurice
Hurt, Jesse

1938 Scores

Morgan	Opponent	Scores
22	Howard	0
0	Union	0
21	Lincoln	0
6	Bluefield	0
12	A&T 0	1
9	Hampton	7
0	VA State	15

1939 Scores Morgan Opponent Scores 0 Union 6 0 Lincoln

1939 Football Team

Bowie, Embra
Kane, John
Brandon, Elisha
Kee, Horace
Brown, Kenneth
Mallory, Ober
Bundy, William
Mosby, Wallace
Burdnell, Stanley
McEwen, Paul
Cain, William
Nickens, Laws
Chavies, Isaac
Ramseur, Erwin
Crippen, Earle

Robinson, Walter
Hampton, Pierce
Smith, Robert
Holley, Wayman
Stevenson, James
Holt, Robert
Threadgill, Harold
Hunt, Leon
Tucker, Maurice
Hurt, Jesse
Watkins, Norman
Johnston, Edward
Webb, James

1939 Scores

Morgan	Opponent	Scores
0	Union	6
0	Lincoln	7
6	Bluefield	6
39	Howard	0
0	A&T	0
7	Hampton	6
0	VA State	3

1940 Football Team

Blackburn, Robert
Holt, Robert
Bowie, Embra
Hunt, Leon
Brandon, Elisha
Hutchinson, Paul
Brickey, Joseph
Kane, John
Brown, Kenneth
Kee, Horace
Buncy, Roy
Lewis, Mack
Burdnell, Stanley
Lewis, Webster
Byron, Cyril
Mosby, Wallace
Cain, William
Nickens, Laws
Campbell, Jonathan
Porter, Henry
Cordington, Wesley

Robinson, Walter
Dodson, Spencer
Rogers, Roland
Drake, Robert
Smith, Robert
Duncan, Robert
Stewart, Carstell
Eggleston, Joseph
Thomas, Lorenzo
Fauntleroy, Authur
Thomas, Luther
Gittens, George
Threadgill, Harold
Givens, Oscar
Tuten, Marvin
Grimsley, Preston
Warner, Joseph
Hampton, Pierce
Webb, James
Henderson, Robert
Webb, Noah

1940 Scores

Morgan	Opponent	Scores
22	Union	0
32	Lincoln	7
21	Bluefield	0
44	Howard	6
34	A&T	0
0	Hampton	0
12	VA State	0

1941 Football Team

Ballard, Reginald
Grimsley, Preston
Threadgill, Harold
Bingham, Edgar
Gross, Charles
Webb, James
Burdnell, Stanley
Hurtt, Melvin
Webb, Noah
Byron, Cyril
Hutchingson, Paul
Whittingham, Mitchell
Campbell, Jonathan
Jackson, Willard
Codington, Wesley
James, Albert
Couch, Flan

Kane, John
Drake, Robert
Marschall, Edward
Duncan, Robert
Mosby, Wallace
Eggleston, Joseph
Porter, Henry
Fauntleroy, Arthur
Rightful, James
Frazier, Charles
Stewart, Carstell
Gaines, Clarence
Thomas, Lorenzo
Givens, Oscar
Thomas, Luther

1941 Scores

Morgan	Opponent	Scores
25	Union	0
14	Lincoln	0
31	Bluefield	0
12	Smith	2
38	A&T	6
6	Hampton	8
19	VA State	6

1942 Football Team

Ballard, Reginald
Givens, Oscar
Thomas, Luther
Black, Joseph
Grimsley, Preston
Turpin, James
Brown, Alvin
Hurtt, Melvin
Webb, Noah
Brown, Oliver
Jackson, Willard
Whittingham, Mitchell
Burgess, Frederick
Kee, Victor
Campbell, Jonathan
McDaniels, Charles

Cawthorne, Leroy
Parker, Stonewall
Chavis, Carl
Porter, Henry
Cordington, Wesley
Rahming, Eugene
Couch, Flan
Robinson, Wade
Duncan, Robert
Slaughter, Clarence
Eggleston, Joseph
Smith, Robert
Frazier, Charles
Stewart, Carstell
Gaines, Clarence
Thomas, Lorenzo

1942 Scores

Morgan	Opponent	Scores
35	Union	7
42	Lincoln	0
6	Bluefield	6
0	Smith	6
9	A&T	0
24	Hampton	3
30	VA State	0

1943 Football Team

Beckett, Stanley
Harris, Elmore
Poag, John
Boone, Joseph
Irvin, Clavin
Rahming, Eugene
Brown, Alvin
Joiner, Hugey
Redd, Rudolph
Burgess, Frederick
Jones, Edward
Redmond, Kenneth
Couch, Flanagan
Jones, Willard

Stansbury, George
Day, Terry
Layton, Melvin
Thomas, Luther
Ellis, Reese
Marshall, Granville
Tyler, Joseph
Frazier, Charles
Moore, Lawrence
Washington, George
Grimsley, Preston
Ogle, Francis
Williams, John

1943 Scores

Morgan	Opponent	Score
25	Camp Holabird	0
43	Wilberforce	0
50	Florida A&M	0
2	Hampton	0
46	VA State	0

1944 Football Team

Berry, Arthur
Ford, Leonard
McNeill, Kenneth
Bond, Paul
Frazier, Charles
Moore, Laurence
Boyce, McDonald
Gaines, Clarence
Poag, John
Brown, Alvin
Harris, Oscar
Rahming, Eugene
Burgess, Frederick
Johnson, Charles
Redmond, Kenneth
Burke, Allen

Joiner, Hugey
Ritchie, Eugene
Carter, Raymond
Jones, Edward
Simpson, Robert
Coppock, Bertram
Jones, Willard
Thomas, Luther
Day, Terry
Kelly, Earl
Thompson, Samuel
Dismond, Horace
Lewis, Napoleon
Watkins, George
Dorsey, Millard

1944 Scores

Morgan	Opponent	Score
47	DE State	0
39	Camp McCall	0
58	Lincoln	0
13	A&T	0
0	Tuskegee AAF	2
55	Hampton	0
6	VA State	3

1945 Football Team
Names and Scores
Not Available

1946 Football Team

Berry, Arthur
Day, Terry
Matthews, Robert
Bingham, Wilford
Eggleston, Joseph
Nelson, Athelson
Black, Joseph
Fauntleroy, Arthur
Nelson, James
Boyce, McDonald
Freeman, Kenneth
Reid, Emmett
Brightful, James
Ghant, William
Ross, James
Brown, Oliver
Gilbert, Albert
Taylor, Marvin
Burley, Bernard
Givens, Oscar
Taylor, Roland H.
Byron, Cyril
Hubberd, Oliver
Thomas, Lorenzo
Campbell, Jonathan
Hurtt, Melvin
Turpin, James
Carter, Raymond
Jones, Edward
Tyler, Lester
Clay, Jesse
Jones, Willard
Ward, Raymond
Cordrington, Wesley
Johnson, Charles
Watkins, George
Coleman, Robert
Kane, John
Whaley, Marvin
Coppock, Bertram
Kelson, Thomas
White, Elwood
Couch, Earl
Lattimer, James
Whittinghamn, Mitchell
Cragway, Roy
Marshall, Augustus
Williams, John M.

1946 Scores

Morgan	Opponent	Score
22	DE State	6
13	WV State	12
35	Grambling Col.	0
28	Lincoln	0
12	A&T 7	1
5	Bluefield	6
20	Hampton	0
6	VA State	0

1947 Football Team

Bank, Theron
Gethers, Noah
Palmer, Warren
Bingham, Edgar
Ghant, William
Priest, James
Black, Joseph
Gilbert, Albert
Rich, Arthur
Brightful, James
Grant, James
Rooks, George
Brown, Oliver
Graves, Howard
St. Thomas, Leroy
Burndnell, Stanley
Hammond, Raymond
Stewart, Jaddie
Burley, Bernard
Harris, William
Stokes, Arthur
Clark, James
Hubbard, Oliver
Turpin, James
Coleman, Earl
Hurtt, Melvin
Tyler, Joseph
Coleman, Robert
Johnson, Charles
Tuten, Marvin
Cragway, Roy
Jones, Edward
Walker, Patrick
Dismond, Horace
Jones, Leon
Ward, Raymond
Duncan, Robert
Kelson, Thomas
White, Elwood
Evans, Eugene
Matthews, Robert
Whaley, Marvin
Fauntleroy, Arthur
Nelson, Athleston
Whittingham, Mitchell
Freeman, Kenneth
Nelson, James C.
Young, Russell

1947 Scores

Morgan	Opponent	Score
31	DE State	0
19	NC State	6
6	Howard	14
14	Lincoln	7
12	A&T	12
13	Bluefield	0
9	Hampton	0
0	VA State	23

1948 Football Team

Anderson, Milton
Baxter, Augustus
Berry, Arthur
Boone, J. Herbert
Brice, Rugherford
Brightful, James
Burley, Bernard
Byrd, Earl
Carter, Raymond
Clark, James
Coleman, Earl
Cragway, Roy
Curtis, Ernest
DePass, Howard
Evans, Eugene
Freeman, Kenneth
Gilbert, Albert
Grant, James
Hammond, Raymond
Harrell, J.C.
Harris, William
Hasty, Thomas
Henderson, Tillman
Howard, Eli
Hubbard, Oliver
Jackson, Joseph
Kelson, Thomas
Lyons, Clarence
Matthews, Robert
Moat, Clifford
Nelson, Athelstan
Palmer, Warren
Priest, James
Robertson, A. B.
Robinson, Cleon
Rooks, George
St. Thomas, Leroy
Stokes, Arthur
Taylor, Roland
Thompson, Willard
Triplett, John
Tuten, Marvin
Walker, Patrick
Whaley, Marvin
White, Elwood
Williams, John
Young, Russell

1948 Scores

Morgan	Opponent	Score
13	NC College	14
41	Delaware	0
12	Lincoln	19
0	A&T	6
46	Bluefield	0
34	Hampton	0
19	VA State	7
13	Howard	2

1949 Football Team

Anderson, Milton
Jackson, Joseph
Banks, Theron
Locust, Irvin
Baxter, Augustus
Mack, James
Brice, Rugherford
Marcus, Matthew
Brown, Roosevelt
Matthews, Robert
Burley, Bernard
Moat, Clifford
Byrd, Earl
Nelson, Athelstan
Clark, James
Palmer, John
Coleman, Earl

Palmer, Warren
Custis, Ernest
Priest, James
Daniels, Joseph
Quann, Howard
DePass, Howard
Robertson, A. B.
Evans, Eugene
Robinson, Chalres
Freeman, Kenneth
Robinson, Cleon
Fugett, Jean
Rooks, George
Gilbert, Albert
Smith, Paul
Harrell, J. C.
Stewart, Edward

Harris, Richard
St. Thomas, Leroy
Harris, William
Taylor, Roland
Hasty, Thomas
Triplett, John
Henderson, Tillman
Young, Russell
Howard, Eli
Whaley, Marvin
Hubbard, Oliver
White, Elwood

1949 Scores

Morgan	Opponent	Score
32	DE	0
19	NC College	7
39	Howard	0
35	Lincoln	0
27	A&T	6
14	Wilberforce	13
26	Hampton	0
34	VA State	7

1950 Football Team

Anthony, Douglas
Holley, Timothy
Banks, Theron
Howard, Eli
Bishop, William
Jackson, Joseph
Brown, Leon
Jones, Freddie
Brown, Roosevelt
Lindsay, Earnest
Buford, William
Locust, Irvin
Byrd, Earl
Jack, James
Clark, James
Marcus, Matthew
Custis, Ernest
Mitchell, Frank
Daniels, Joseph
Quann, Howard
Davis, Jonas

Robbins, Walter
De Pass, Howard
Robertson, A. B.
Evans, Eugene
Robinson, Charles
Faulkner, John
Rooks, George
Fox, Melvin
St. Thomas, Leroy
Fugett, Jean
Steward, Edward
Green, James
Stokes, Arthur
Hammond, Raymond
Thompson, William
Harrell, J. C.
Triplett, John
Harrell, Lawrence
Tuten, Marvin
Harrington, Betram

Weaver, Charles
Harris, Richard
Williams, George
Harris, William
Young, Russell
Hasty, Thomas
Henderson, Tillman

1950 Scores

Morgan	Opponent	Score
20	DE	0
42	Lincoln	14
32	Howard	0
6	WV State	6
0	A&T	0
14	Wilberforce	12
27	Hampton	13
14	VA State	7

1951 Football Team

Banks, Theron	Mosley, Robert	Triplett, John
Hurtz, John	Davis, Jonas	Henderson, Tillman
Bishop, William	Patterson, Donald	White, Stanley
Jennings, Albert	DePass, Howard	Holley, Timothy
Brown, Roosevelt	Perry, Robert	Williams, George
Johnson, Otis	Fields, James	Holt, William
Buford, William	Quann, Howard	Wright, Bennie
Jones, Earl	Freeman, Gary	
Byrd, Earl	Robbins, Walter	
Jordon, Milton	Fox, Melvin	
Cassidy, Joseph	Ross, Donald	
Lindsay, Ernest	Green, James	
Carr, Walter	Stern, Oliver	
Locust, Irvin	Harrell, Lawrence	
Covert, Edgar	Steward, Edward	
Marcus, Matthew	Harris, Richard	
Cropper, Walter	Stokes, Arthur	
Morton, Robert	Hasty, Thomas	
Daniels, Joseph		

1951 Scores

Morgan	Opponent	Score
45	Delaware	6
7	Lincoln	2
14	Howard	0
13	WV State	20
6	A&T	31
6	Hampton	7
8	VA State	14

1952 Football Team

Austin, James
Bishop, William
Brown, Roosevelt
Buford, William
Cassidy, Joseph
Chapman, Donald
Cropper, Roland
Covert, Edgar, B.
Covert, Robert
Davis, Jonas
Freeman, Gary
Gaines, Alfred
Gamble, James
Gibson, Carroll
Graham, Pasley
Green, James
Harrell, Lawrence
Hartsfield, Howard
Holley, Timothy
Hughes, Hugh P.
Johnson, Otis
Locust, Irvin
Lindsay, Ernest
Marcus, Mathew
Martin, George
McKinney, George
Miles, Jesse
Mosley, Walter
Morton, Robert
Murray, Theodore
Patterson, Donald
Perguson, Douglas
Prather, Gilbert
Quann, Howard
Randall, Leonard
Robbins, Walter
Scott, Arthur
Scott, Edward
Scott, John
Smith, Guy Paul
Ware, John Charles
Williams, George
White, Stanley J.
Whitted, Carl

1953 Football Team
Names and Scores Not Available

1954 Football Team
Names and Scores Not Available

1955 Football Team

Austin, James
McArthur, Jerome
Billups, William
McCoy, Benjamin
Brooks, Joseph
Miles, Jesse
Buckson, Jospeh
Porter, Charles
Chapman, Donald
Prather, Gilbert A.
Clark, William
Pratt, William M.
Courtney, James
Reinhardt, Charles
Dean, Arthur
Rowe, Albert
Dorsey, James
Rozier, Jackson
Doub, Frank
Ruff, George
Evans, Charles

Sewell, John
Gordon, William
Smith, Gilbert
Hamwright, Charles
Smith, Henry
Hawkins, Clarence
Stewart, LeBaron
Haywood, James
Thomas, Stephen
Jacobs, Robert
White, Robert
Jones, Earl
Williams, Dolphus
Lewis, James
Yorke, Robert

1955 Scores

Morgan	Opponent	Score
19	Central State	7
13	Morris Brown	18
32	Howard	0
6	WV State	0
0	A&T College	14
19	VA Union U	6
45	Hampton	7
32	VA State	19

1956 Football Team
Names and Scores Not Available

1957 Football Team Names not available

1957 Scores

Morgan	Opponent	Score
0	Howard	48
0	WV State	33
12	NC A&T	13
6	Hampton	25
40	VA State	14
23	Central State	7
7	Union	13
27	NC College	7
7	MD State	7

1958 Football Team

Allen, James	Hart, Donald
Bell, Thomas	Hawkins, Clarence
Bowen, Earl	Haywood, James
Brown, Albert	Manning, John
Buffaloe, Lawrence	Mays, Ernest
Butts, Thomas	McLain, Marion
Chase, Ralph	Miller, Ralph
Clark, Phillip	Morgan, Walter
Clay, Eugene	Mosby, Ernest
Crawley, Clarence	Napper, Theodore
Cunningham, Alfred	Perguson, Douglass
Dennis, Jack	Reed, Wyndham
Evans, Loyal	Richards, Henry
Flye, Elmer	Robinson, Homer
Forrest, George	Smart, Lawson
Frier, Samuel	Utley, Robert
Gordon, Bobby	White, Robert
Greene, Fred	White, William
Hairston, James	Whitt, Nonie
Hall, William	Williams, Dolphus
Harris, Arnold	Williams, Lougene
Harris, Samuel	Young, Robert

1958 Scores

Morgan	Opponent	Score
48	Howard	0
6	WV State	8
2	NC A&T	20
60	Hampton	0
20	VA State	6
69	VA Union	0
7	NC College	14
13	MD State	12

1959 Football Team
(Hurt's Last Year)

Alford, Robert
Allen, James
Alston, Herbert
Benjamin, George
Binion, Russell
Bowen, Earl T.
Brown, Albert L.
Brown, William C.
Chase, Ralph
Clark, Phillip
Clay, Eugene
Cole, Wayne
Crawley, Clarence
Cunningham, Alfred
Forrest, George
Frier, Samuel
Gibson, Joseph
Hairston, James
Hall, William G.
Harper, David
Hite, Carl
Hunter, Michael
Jackson, Allen
Jackson, Robert
Johnson, Leslie
Johnson, Vernon
Kornegay, James
Lewis, James E.
McGhee, Howard
McLain, Marion
Manning, John
Miller, Ralph
Mitchell, Clarence
Nesbitt, David
Pergerson, Douglas
Pompey, Carmie
Reed, Donald
Reed, Freddie
Richardson, George
Robinson, Homer
Rogers, George
Royster, Robert
Sartor, Frank
Smith, Carl
Smith, Harold
Smith, Louis
Utley, Robert
Whitt, Nonie
Young, Robert

1959 Scores

Morgan	Opponent	Score
14	Howard	0
6	WV State	6
8	NC A&T	40
6	Hampton	9
7	VA State	12
9	VA Union	14
10	NC College	12
7	MD State	20

Swimming
1952
1953
1955
1956

1952, 1953, 1955, 1956 Swimming Team

Barnes, Hubert
Barton, Boyce
Bates, Luther
Bishop, Douglass
Brooks, Joseph
Brown, Clarence
Brown, William
Cash, Robert
Clark, Cecil
Cooper, Cecil
Dalton, William
Diggs, Clarence
Dillingham, Donald
Dixon, Donald
Dorsey, Maurice
Douglas, George
Fulcher, Walter
Garlington, David
Graham, Kenneth
Gumbs, Selvin
Harris, Arnold
Hendrick, Jay

Hobson, Burleigh
Holley, Richard
Howard, Daniel
Jackson, Waverly
Jenkins, Aaron
Jones, Andrew
Jones, Maurice
Jones, Martin
Jones, Robert L.
Kelly, Charles
Lee, Landis
Montgomery, Lawrence
Newton, James
Rawlings, Wilbur
Rice, Herbert
Tarter, Donald
Tucker, Donald
Walker, David
Warren, James
Williams, John

Boxing

1940 Boxers

Brandon, Elisha   McQwen, Paul   Winston, Charles

1947 & 1948 Boxers

Cousins, Furrie
Freeman, Arthur
Hackley, Calvin
Murdock, John
Poag, John
Wadley, James
Brown, Wilbur
Goldsly, Clarence
Hasty, Theodore
Rooks, George
Milner, Theodore
Spruiella Rufus
White, Richard

1949 & 1950 Boxers

Dorsey, Daniel
Eubanks, John
Faulkner, John
Fox, Melvin
Green, Francies
Godsly, Clarence
Graves, Bennie
Hasty, Thomas
Lindsay, Ernest
Rogers, Ralph
Spruiella, Rufus
White, Richard

1952, 1953, 1954, & 1955 Boxers

Brown, Roosevelt
Brown, Thomas
Dorsey, David
Eubanks, John
Faulk, Ronald
Gibbs, James
Graham, Pasley
Harrell, Lawrence
Harrington, Bertram
Hughes, James
Johnson, Parish
Lindsay, Ernest
Moore, Samuel
Morton, Earl
Parson, Charles
Pumphrey, Nathaniel
Williams, David
Williams, John
Wilson, Wesley
Banks, Charles
Brown, William
Carter, Vernon
Mello, Earl
Randall, Fred
White, Willis
William, Caseo

1956 & 1957 Boxers

Carter, Vernon
Craig, Ronald
Cummings, William
Dawthord, Clarence
Heyliger, James
Key, Willie
Kcys, James
Pannell, Patrick
Payne, Samuel
Rogers, Alonzo
Shivers, Richard
Wallace, John

Wrestling

1940-41 Wrestling

Brown, Kenneth
Campbell, Jonathan
Tennessee, Paul

1942 Wrestling

Ballard, Reginald
Campbell, Jonathan

1947-48 Wrestling

Boston, Joseph
Burley, Bernard
Campbell, Jonathan
White, Clay
Fauntelroy, Arthur
Fraling, Matthew
Gilbert, Albert
Graves, Howard
Hill, Donald
Hoff, Nat
Jones, Earl
Jones, John
Mitchener, Charles
Ward, Raymond

1950, 1952, 1953, & 1955 Wrestling

Brown, Roosevelt
Brown, Thomas
Carey, Donald
Clement, George
Dorsey, David
Eubanks, John
Faulk, Ronald
Frailing, Matthew
Gibbs, James
Graham, Pasley
Harrell, Lawrence
Hawkins, Milton
Hemmings, Kenneth
Hoff, Nathaniel
Holley, Richard
Hughes, James
Johnson, Parish
Jubilee, Eugene
Lindsay, Ernest
McDaniel, Moses
Merris, Joseph
Moore, Samuel
Morton, Earl
Moulton, Samuel
Parson, Charles
Pope, Jesse
Raymond, Lawrence
Rice, David
Robinson, John
Spivey, George
Sturdivant, Willie
Whaley, George
Williams, David
Williams, Earl
Williams, Harold
Williams, John
Wilson, Wesley
Wyatt, Littleton

Tennis

1931-32 Tennis Team

Burton, Lawrence
Jones, Edward
Johnson, Alva

1937, 1940, 1941 Tennis Team

Allen, Hayes
Carter, Simon
Shephard, Milton
Smith, Hugh
Cole, Harry
Weave, Warren
Yearwood, Eddie

1948-1949 Tennis Team

Boston, Joe
Coleman, Edward
Farley, Ronald
Finch, Earl
Freeman, Kenneth
Holland, Henry
Johnson, Charles
Jubilee, Benjamin
Lee, Eugene
Parham, Joe

1952 Tennis Team

Bondurant, Frank
Bowser, Leon
Brooks, Robert
Butler, Albert
Colbert, Norman
Fox, Melvin
Murphy, Raymond
Wallace, Edward

1955, 1956, & 1957 Tennis Team

Bowser, Leon
Hayes, Charles
Koger, Earl
Murphy, Raymond
Thompson, Frank
Williams, Conrad

Basketball Players

1931 Basketball Team

1931 Scores

Morgan	Opponent	Scores
37	Lincoln	30
39	Howard	20
27	Lincoln	14
38	Howard	24
74	Shaw	23
73	Shaw	13
40	Hampton	26
55	VA State	18
91	Livingstone	23
41	VA State	22

Blueford, James
Conrad, Thomas
Gibson, Charles
Jones, Williams E.
Jones, Wilmer
Murdock, Ezra
Roy, Melvin
Waters, Worthington
Wilson, Howard

1932 Basketball Team

1932 Scores

Morgan	Opponent	Scores
47	Union	16
46	St. Paul	26
29	Howard	34
25	VA State	28
36	St. Paul	14
53	Union	36
64	Hampton	23
36	Howard	25
34	VA State	33
45	Lincoln	35

Burton, Lawrence
Conrad, Thomas
Gibson, Charles
Hackett, Rufus
Jones, Wolmer
Knox, Augustus
Rasin, James
Rawlings, Avon
Saunders, Reuben
Troupe, Otis
Waters, Worthington
Wilson, Howard
Williams, James

1933 Basketball Team

1933 Scores

Morgan	Opponent	Scores
40	Bluefield	23
45	Bluefield	32
47	St. Paul	14
47	St. Paul	18
29	VA State	25
49	VA State	31
62	Howard	22
44	Howard	27
41	Lincoln	22
31	Lincoln	19
45	Hampton	33
37	Hampton	36
56	Union	35

Conrad, Thomas
Crawford, Hubert
Dorsey, John
Eaton, Douglas
Gibson, Charles
Hackett, Rufus
Raisin, James
Sturgis, John
Taylor, Paul
Troupe, Otis
Williams, James
Williams, Wendell
Wilson, Howard
Yearwood, Edward
Yearwood, Joseph

1934 Basketball Team

1934 Scores

Morgan	Opponent	Scores
35	Union	24
52	Union	29
29	Howard	25
24	Howard	26
52	Bluefield	34
35	Bluefield	18
36	St. Paul	30
60	St. Paul	24
29	VA State	26
28	VA State	33
15	Hampton	29
38	Hampton	32
29	Lincoln	23
37	Lincoln	32

Conrad, Thomas
Crawford, Hubert
Drake, Carl
Hackett, Rufus
Harmon, Frank
Mosby, Walter
Simpson, William
Sturgis, John
Taylor, Paul
Troupe, Otis
Weaver, Warren
Williams, Edward
Wilson, Howard

1935 Basketball Team

1935 Scores

Morgan	Opponent	Scores
47	Union	51
44	Union	42
45	St. Paul	18
32	St. Paul	28
36	VA State	46
48	VA State	52
36	Hampton	42
34	Lincoln	40
25	Lincoln	37
42	Howard	48
41	Howard	46

Brown, Thomas
Crawford, Hubert
Dorey, John
Drake, Carl
Hawkins, Benjamin
Lampkins, William
Lockwood, Vernell
Simpson, William
Smith, James
Sowell, Richard
Troupe, Otis
Yearwood, Edward
Walker, H. (Manger)

1936 Basketball Team

Anderson, Leonard
Blackwell, Richard
Brown, Thomas
Cheatham, John
Crawford, Hubert
Davis, Wilbert
Dorsey, John
Gordon, Frank S.
Lampkins, William
Lockwood, Vernell
Mitchell, Robert
Mosby, Walter
Ryan, Masso
St. Clair, James
Simpson, William
Smith, James
Sowell, Richard
Weaver, Warren

1936 Scores

Morgan	Opponent	Scores
42	Lincoln	36
24	Lincoln	23

1937 Basketball Team

Brown, Thomas
Cheatham, John
Clarke, Wilbur
Cromwell, Horace
Gordon, Frank
Hampton, Pierce
Grant, George
Hill, Lawrence
Holly, Wayman
Kee, James
Lampkins, William
Lewis, Archibald
Lockwood, Vernell
Mitchell, Robert
Mosby, Walter
Ryans, Maso
Simpson, William
Smith, James
Sowell, Richard

1937 Scores

Morgan	Opponent	Score
25	VA State	24
29	VA State	31
30	Hampton	44
23	Hampton	39
41	Howard	38
37	Howard	38
31	A&T	26
26	A&T	37
28	Union	29
37	Bluefield	20
32	Lincoln	40
56	Smith	37
29	Lincoln	37

1938 Basketball Team

Brown, Thomas
Cain, William
Clark, Wilbur
Gibson, Lionel
Gordon, Frank
Henderson, Robert
Hill, Lawrence
Holley, Wayman
Lampkins, William
Lockwood, Vurnell
Mitchell, Robert
Mosby, Walter
Patterson, Bennie
Richardson, John
Ryans, Maso
Smith, James
Smith, Robert
Sowell, Richard
Watkins, Norman

1938 Scores

Morgan	Opponent	Score
30	N. C. State	22
36	Union	44
43	Hampton	51
40	Lincoln	32
52	Howard	51
39	Howard	37
49	Hampton	27
46	Union	45
42	Smith	40
42	Lincoln	22
38	N.C. State	25
60	Shaw	42
38	A&T	30

1939 Basketball Team

1939 Scores

Morgan	Opponent	Score
44	Smith	39
44	VA State	57
46	Union	45
43	Hampton	44
71	Hampton	40
51	VA State	48
45	Lincoln	38
53	Shaw	48
49	Union	74
65	Bluefield	53
60	A&T	34
69	St. Paul	54
34	Lincoln	50

Ashby, Aubrey
Cain, William
Clarke, Wilbur
Gibson, Linnel
Green, Lawrence
Holley, H. Wayman
Johnston, Edward
Mosby, Wallace
Patterson, Bennie
Ryans, Maso
Smith, Robert
Spaulding, Albert
Watkins, Norman
Webb, James

1940 Basketball Team

1940 Scores

Morgan	Opponent	Score
51	Hampton	39
56	Hampton	49
54	Howard	44
46	Howard	61
36	Lincoln	46
60	Lincoln	59
57	St. Paul	45
56	Smith	43
47	Union	59
38	Union	41
46	VA Sate	40
54	VA State	59

Byron, Cyril
Cain, William
Chavies, Isaac
Dixon, Samuel
Garrison, Madison
Gibson, Lionel
Green, Lawrence
Holley, Wayman
James, Albert
Mosby, Wallace
Richardson, John
Smith, Robert
Spaulding, Albert
Staten, John
Watkins, Norman
Webb, James

1941 Basketball Team

1941 Scores

Morgan	Opponent	Score
52	Hampton	49
41	Howard	32
49	Howard	34
42	Lincoln	35
45	Lincoln	47
38	NC State	48
36	NC State	53
61	Smith	72
48	Smith	53
40	Union	57
33	Union	60
34	VA State	40
45	VA State	43

Byron, Cyril
Cain, William
Dixon, Samuel
Garrison, Madison
Gibson, Lionel
Gittens, George
Givens, Oscar
Hutchingson, Paul
James, Albert
Mosby, Wallace
Smith, Robert
Staten, John
Thomas, Allen
Waters, Alfred
Watkins, Norman

1942 Basketball Team

1942 Scores

Morgan	Opponent	Score
61	Bluefield	47
48	Hampton	40
39	Howard	29
50	Lincoln	45
41	Lincoln	37
26	NC State	40
40	NC State	61
48	Shaw	38
31	Smith	35
48	Smith	57
44	VA State	39
45	VA State	49

Allen, Hayes
Bressant, Leon
Brown, Alvin
Byron, Cyril
Dixon, Samuel
Eggleston, Joseph
Gaines, Clarence
Garrison, Madison
Gittens, George
Givens, Oscar
Hutchingson, Paul
James, Albert
Mosby, Wallace
Smith, Robert
Staten, John
Thomas, Allen
Woods, Aubrey

1943 Basketball Team

Allen, Hayes
Ballard, Reginald
Black, Joseph
Bressant, Leon
Brown, Alvin
Campbell, Jonathan
Ducan, Robert
Eggleston, Joseph
Irvin, Calvin
Gaines, Clarence
Givens, Oscar
Grimsley, Preston
Harden, Louie
Hurt, Melvin
Lee, James
Pinkett, Roberson
Smith, Robert
Woods, Aubrey
Young, Ulysses

1943 Scores

Morgan	Opponent	Score
71	Hampton	48
58	Howard	39
44	Howard	19
47	Lincoln	52
60	Lincoln	42
33	Smith	40
66	VA State	62
43	VA State	53

1944 Basketball Team

Bass, Marshall
Brown, Alvin
Brurke, Allen
Day, Terry
Ellis, Reese
Ford, Leonard
Gaines, Clarence
Grimsley, Preston
Irvin, Calvin
Jones, Edward
Jones, Willard
Pinkett, Grant
Washington, George

1944 Scores

Morgan	Opponent	Score
39	Hampton	42
35	Howard	39
61	Howard	49
39	Lincoln	40
48	Lincoln	51
52	VA State	40
48	VA State	44
51	Union	48
48	Union	47
46	WV State	36
56	WV State	29

1945 Basketball Team

Boyce, MacDonald
Brown, Alvin
Burke, Allen
Carter, Raymond
Copeland, Rowland
Day, Terry
Ford, Leonard
Gaines, Clarence
Irvin, Calvin
Jones, Edward
Jones, Willard
McNeil, Kenneth
Ritchie, Eugene
Ross, Wilbur
Watkins, George

1945 Scores

Morgan	Opponent	Score
67	Bluefield	40
68	DE State	35
67	DE State	49
71	Howard	50
63	Howard	38
48	Lincoln	41
49	Lincoln	27
69	NC State	56
52	NC State	40
61	Smith	35
44	Smith	36
61	VA State	44
60	VA State	35
61	Union	35
64	Union	42

1947 Basketball Team

Beaird, Franklin
Black, Joseph
Bressant, Leon
Copeland, Roland
Day, Terry
Duncan, Robert W.
Eggleston, Joseph
James, Albert
Jones, Ermon
Lattimer, James
Lewis, Webster
Sealey, Ralph
Stewart, Jaddie
Taylor, Roland
Ross, Wilbur
Tillman, Gervis
Trupin, James
Washington, Ernest
Washington, George

1947 Scores

Morgan	Opponent	Score
39	NC State	31
35	NC State	52
57	A&T	54
60	DE State	47
50	Howard	42
52	VA Union	53
55	VA State	46
76	VA State	61
57	Lincoln	44
52	Lincoln	37
39	Lincoln	43
48	Lincoln	38
51	Howard	49
45	DE State	54
50	NC State	48
71	Union	66
49	A&T	41
41	NC State	73

Note: Coach Hill became head basketball coach during the 1947-48 season.

1948 Basketball Team

Bressant, Leon
Duncan, Robert
Evans, Eugene
Fair, Arlo
Harris, David
Harris, William
Howard, Eli
Johnson, Lawrence
Jones, Ermon
Lee, Eugene
Sealey, Ralph
Turpin, James
Vaughters, Thomas
Washington, Earnest
Young, Russell

1948 Scores

Morgan	Opponent	Score
56	VA State	73
76	JC Smith	53
45	DE State	70
32	Howard	45
28	VA Union	29
48	VA State	38
44	NC College	56
36	Shaw	25
61	Lincoln	54
63	NC College	53
50	Howard	54
54	Shaw	35
42	VA Union	52
62	DE State	72
41	Lincoln	50

1949 Basketball

Byrd, Earl
Edmonds, John
Fair, Arlo
Liston, George
Harris, David
Harris, William
Henderson, Tillman
Howard, Eli
Johnson, Laurence
Moat, Clifford
Peters, Edmund
Sealey, Ralph
Taylor, Roland
Thompson, Willard
Triplett, John
Vaughters, Thomas
Washington, Ernest
Washington, George
Young, Russell

1949 Scores

Morgan	Opponent	Score
48	Wilmington	39
39	MD State	57
45	NC College	55
79	Wilmington	45
72	DE State	61
31	Lincoln	40
52	DE State	61
76	Morgan St. Alumni	67
40	Howard	54
43	VA Union	64
48	VA State	52
49	NC College	58
66	NC A&T	58
48	Hampton	50
58	VA State	66
66	NC College	65
62	Howard	61
60	VA Union	55
75	Lincoln	57
67	NC A&T	56
58	Hampton	50
73	Winston-Salem	60
84	MD State	82
47	VA Union	63

1950 Basketball Team

Bright, Nathan
Byrd, Earl
Edmonds, John
Fair, Arlo
Harris, David
Harris, William
Henderson, Tillman
Howard, Eli
Johnson, Lawrence
Miller, Carl
Redd, Eugene
Sealey, Ralph
Taylor, Ronald
Stepto, Herman
Tolson, Lewis
Thweatt, Robert
Young, Russell

1950 Scores

Morgan	Opponent	Score
56	VA Union	62
56	VA Union	65
51	VA State	50
55	VA State	68
59	NC College	61
53	NC College	92
71	JC Smith	91
47	JC Smith	53
50	Howard	57
45	Howard	53
62	Winston-Salem	61

1951 Basketball Team

Barricks, Charles
Battle, Joe
Bell, Carl
Childs, Avon
Covert, John
Douglas, Robert
Epps, James
Gardner, Lester
Garrett, Ernest
Graves, Erwin R.
Hanes, Edward
Harrison, Charles
Heartley, Harvey
Hill, Talmadge L.
Hudson, Ralph
Johnson, Aaron
Jones, Sam
Lipscomb, Donald
Lowery, Maurice
Mackell, John
McClaren, Fred
McMillian, Charles
McQueen, George
Murphy, Raymond
Perry, Norman
JayRobinson
Rogers, Thomas
Roseborough, Arthur
Spry, Lehman
Thweatt, Robert
Tipton, Thomas
Wade, Herman
Walton, Rawlins
Warlick, Ernest
Wells, Lester
Whitted, Carl
Williams, George
Winestock, Mark

1951 Scores

Morgan	Opponent	Score
67	Lincoln	71
58	Howard	60
82	DE State	73
64	Howard	50
64	Hampton	50
84	Hampton	81
60	VA Union	82
76	VA State	83
77	Winston-Salem	70
75	NC College	78
64	VA Union	67
74	Lincoln	66
77	Shaw	63
73	VA State	59
97	DE State	55

1952 Basketball Team

Bright, Nathan
Colbert, Robert
Gardner, Lester
Garrett, Ernest
Hill, Talmadge, Jr.
Hudson, Ralph
McMillian, Charles
Murphy, Raymond
Roseborough, Arthur
Spry, Lehman
Thweatt, Robert
Wells, Lester
Whitted, Carl
Williams, George

1952 Scores

Morgan	Opponent	Score
65	Morgan St. Alumni	40
100	Miner Teachers	54
84	Hampton, Institute	68
81	Lincoln	56
67	Howard	58
76	DE State	52
73	Hampton Institute	81
107	St. Paul's	87
77	VA State	83
65	VA Union	66
111	Lincoln	67
74	JC Smith	93
57	Loyola	64
74	VA State	41
61	VA Union	57
92	DE State	90
82	Howard	66
74	Hampton	70
50	Winston-Salem	51
95	JC Smith	69

1954 Basketball Team

Barksdale, Robert
Davis, Clayton
Ford, James
Garner, Ronald
Garrett, Ernest
Hicks, James
Hill, Talmadge, Jr.
Long, James
McMillian, Charles
Marshall, Kenneth
Moore, Allan
Murphy, Raymond
Ranson, Arnold
Rozier, Jackson
Sharpe, Ronald
Wells, Lester

1954 Scores

Morgan	Opponent		Score
69	Fayetteville St.		59
79	Hampton Institute		93
77	Hampton Institute		60
88	Howard		81
93	Howard		78
64	JC Smith		78
78	JC Smith		77
63	Lincoln		47
96	Lincoln		75
74	MD State		77
101	A&T		94
82	A&T		72
104	NC College		79
73	St. Paul's		82
79	St. Paul's		54
77	VA State	81	
88	VA State	77	
64	VA Union		76
75	VA Union		91

1956 Basketball Team

Barber, Leroy
Barksdale, Robert
Brightful, Charles
Briscoe, Thomas
Duren, Edward
Froe, Dana
Garner, Ronald
Gray, Walter L.
Gross, Ronald
Hudgins, Eugene
Jackson, Samuel
Johnson, Aaron
Lawson, Floyd
Long, James
Lyght, Williams
Middleton, Ernest
Moore, Allan
Rozier, Jackson
Smith, Henry E.
White, John

1956 Scores

Morgan	Opponent	Score
77	WV State	72
75	Elizabethtown	70
80	VA Union	71
82	Hampton Institute	73
79	NC College	84
68	MD State	74
70	Howard	58
85	A&T	91
75	Hampton	69
69	VA State	75
72	VA Union	88
79	Lincoln	54
54	NC College	67
52	A&T	60
72	VA State	58
71	MD State	80
96	Lincoln	54
69	Winton-Salem Teachers	65
77	Howard	61
62	A&T	70

Track

1931-32 Track Team

Cottman, Alphonso
Bell, Alfred
Conrad, Thomas
Gibbs, James
Grant, James
Hammond, Wiley
Johnson, Andrew
Lowery, Reginald
Spencer, James
Sterling, Russell
Taylor, Clinton
Thompson, Robert
Troupe, Otis
Williams, Wendell

1933-34 Track Team

Byrd, Eugene
Conrad, Thomas
Cottman, Alphonso
Daye, Cornell
Drake, Carl
Johnson, Andrew
Jordan, Wilbur
Gibbs, James
Lowery, Reginald
Mosby, Walter
Preston, Lester
Simpson, William
Sturgis, John
Troupe, Otis
Waters, Eldridge
Williams, Wendell
Wynder, John

1935 Track Team

Barrow, Arthur
Brown, Thomas
Byrd, Eugene
Calhoun, Jack
Callaman, Melvin
Campbell, Preston
Chester, Frederick
Drake, Carl
Gibbs, James
Hawkins, Benjamin
Jordan, Wilbur
Knightin, Claiborne
Lampkins, William
Lowery, Reginald
Preston, Lester
Roberts, Douglass
Roberts, Richard
Smith, James
Sowell, Richard
Spencer, Norris
Wynder, John

1936 Track Team

Blanks, George
Callaman, Melvin
Cheatham, John
Davis, James
Davis, Wilbert
Drake, Carl
Gordon, Frank
Hardin, Herbert
Hawkins, Benjamin
Jordan, J. Wilbur (Capt.)

Maiden, Clarence
McCoy, Armand
Mosby, Walter
Ross, Nolan
Ross, Wellington
Ryan, Maso
Smith, James
Simpson, William
Troupe, Otis

1937 Track Team

Callaman, Melvin
Cheatham, John
Chester, Frederick
Cromwell, Horace
Davis, James
Fletcher, John
Gordon, Frank
Holly, Wayman
Hurt, Jesse
Kee, James
Magee, William
Maiden, Clarence
Mosby, Walter
Robinson, Walter
Ross, Nolan
Ross, Wellington
Ryan, Maso
Simpson, William
Smith, James
Sowell, Richard
Wilson, John

1938 Track Team

Bowie, Embra
Brown, Kenneth
Callaman, Melvin
Gordon, Frank
Holly, Wayman
Hurt, Jesse
Kee, James
Magee, William
Maiden, Clarence
Mosby, Walter
Robinson, Walter
Ross, Wellington
Ryans, Maso
Smith, James
Smith, Reuben
Thomas, James
Watson, Edward

1939 Track Team

Bowie, Embra
Brandon, Elisha
Brown, Kenneth
Bundy, William
Cain, William
Clarke, James
Daly, Richard
Fletcher, John
Hampton, Pierce
Holley, Wayman
Holt, Robert
Hurt, Jesse
Johnson, Roy
Kee, Horace
Lindsay, Robert

Magee, William
Ross, Wellington
Watson, Edward

1940 Track Team

Andrews, Robert
Bowie, Embra
Brandon, Elisha
Burdnell, Stanley
Byron, Cyril
Cain, William
Clarke, James
Crippen, Earl
Fassett, James
Fletcher, John
Garrison, Madison
Hampton, Pierce
Holley, Wayman
Hurt, Jesse
Kee, Horace
Magee, William
Watson, Edward
Webb, James

1941 Track Team

Bowie, Embra
Brown, Kenneth
Burdnell, Stanley
Byron, Cyril
Cain, William
Campbell, Jonathan
Cordrinton, Wesley
Covington, Robert
Drake, Robert
Fletcher, John

Garrison, Madison
Gittings, George
Hampton, Herbert
Holt, Robert
Hurtt, Melvin
Kee, Horace
Lewis, Webster
Smith, Hugh
Stewart, Carstell
Thomas, Allen
Thomas, Lorenzo
Thomas, Luther
Trader, David

1942 Track Team

Ballard, Reginald
Bingham, Edgar
Brown, Herman
Codrington, Wesley
Campbell, Jonathan
Daly, Edwin
Drake, Robert
Eggleston, Joseph
Givens, Oscar
Hurtt, Melvin
Kee, Victor
Mosby, Wallace
Porter, Henry
Stewart, Carstell
Thomas, Allen
Thomas, Lorenzo
Trader, Davis

1943 Track Team

Black, Joseph
Campbell, Jonathan
Davis, Marvin
Gaines, Clarence
Harden, Louie
Pinkett, Grant
Poag, John
Redd, Rudolph
Stanbury, George
Trader, David
Walton, Reginald

1944 Track Team

Bond, Paul
Coppock, Bertram
Day, Terry
Harris, Elmore
Hugey, Joiner
Lewis, Napoleon
Poag, John
Redd, Rudolph
Thomas, Luther
Trader, David

1945 Track Team

Bond, Paul
Bruce, Harry
Coppock, Bertram
Dismond, Horace
Joiner, Hugey
Lewis, Napoleon
Nelson, James C.
Poag, Thomas

Priest, James
Ritchie, Eugene
Ross, Wilbur
Thomas, Luther
Thompson, Samuel
Williams, David
Williams, James

1946 Track Team

Black, Joseph
Bishop, William
Bond, Paul
Brent, William
Brown, William
Bruce, Harry
Campbell, Jonathan
Coppock, Bertram
Costen, Samuel
Crooms, John
Dismond, Horace
Dixon, Kenneth
Gross, Harry
Harden, Louie
Hubbard, Oliver
Hurt, Melvin
Johnson, David
Joiner, Hugey
Lewis, Napoleon
Morris, Marshall
Nelson, James C.
Penny, Milton
Poag, Thomas
Priest, James
Rich, Arthur
Ritchie, Eugene
Ross, Wilbur
Stewart, Carstell

Thomas, Luther
Thompson, Samuel
Tyler, Robert
Vaughters, Thomas
Whaley, Marvin
White, Elwood
Williams, David
Williams, James

1947 Track Team

Black, Joseph
Bishop, William
Bond, Paul
Brent, William
Brown, William
Campbell, Jonathan
Costen, Samuel
Crooms, John
Dixon, Kenneth
Gross, Harry
Harden, Louie
Hubbard, Oliver
Hurtt, Melvin
Johnson, David
Morris, Marshall
Nelson, James C.
Penny, Milton
Poag, Thomas
Priest, James
Rich, Arthur
Ross, Wilbur
Stewart, Carstell
Tyler, Robert
Vaughters, Thomas
Whaley, Marvin
White, Elwood
Williams, David

1948 Track Team

Adams, William
Baxter, William
Brent, William
Brooks, William
Brown, Thurlow
Brown, William
Campbell, Jonathan
Costen, Samuel
Crooms, John
Dixon, Kenneth
Gee, Ronald
Graham, Robert
Gross, Harry
Hardin, Louie
Haynes, Robert
Hubbard, Oliver
LaBeach, Samuel
Lipscomb, Christopher
Moat, Clifford
Morris, Marshall
Robinson, Bernard
Scott, Lester
St. Thomas, Leroy
Triplett, John
Tuten, Thomas
Tyler, Robert
Vaugherts, Thomas
West, George
White, Elwood

1949 Track Team

Adams, William
Baxter, William
Bragg, Arthur
Brent, William
Brooks, William
Brooks, George
Brown, Thurlow
Brown, William
Campbell, Claybrooke
Carpenter, Robert
Costen, Samuel
Crooms, John
Dixon, Kenneth
Gardner, James
Gee, Ronald
Gooden, Louis
Graham, Robert
Gross, Harry
Hardin, Louie
Haynes, Robert
Hubbard, Oliver
Jefferson, George
LaBeach, Byron
LaBeach, Samuel
Lipscombe, Christopher
Moat, Clifford
Morgan, Howard
Morris, Marshall
Murray, James
Peaker, Alexander
Quann, Howard
Rhoden, George
Robinson, Bernard
Robinson, Cleon
Scott, Lester
St. Thomas, Leroy

Thomas, Eugene
Triplett, John
Tuten, Marvin
Tyler, Robert
Vaughters, Thomas
Welch, Alfred
West, George
White, Elwood

1951, 1952 & 1953 Track Team

Bosmond, Bernard
Bragg, Arthur
Breedlove, Bertram
Brown, Leon
Carr, Walter
Culbreath, Joshua
Davis, John
Freeman, Walter
Gee, Ronald
Gooden, Louis
Griffen, Lawrence
Henley, Donald
Henriquez, Joseph
Holley, Timothy
Hunt, Samuel
John, Vincent
Johnson, Otis
Kave, Kenneth
Kess, Leon
LaBeach, Bryon
LaBeach, Samuel
Lee, Nathan
Mills, Charles
Morgan, Howard
Mitchell, Frank

Murray, Theodore
Quann, Howard
Rhoden, George
Robinson, Bernard
Robinson, Robert
Rogers, James
Scott, Lester
Smith, Donald
Street, Clover
Thomas, Eugene
Thompson, Lancelot
Thompson, William
Tinson, Ronald
Triplett, John
Tuten, Marvin
Wade, Herman
Washington, Herbert
Waters, Edward
Welch, Alfred
Williams, George
Wright, Bennie

(Note: Names of 1954 track members not available. See 1953-55 lists.)

1955, 1956, & 1957 Track Team

Armstrong, Paul
Barksdale, Robert
Barry, Juanito
Berry, Robert
Bolden, Herbert
Brown, Roland
Buffaloe, Lawrence
Bumford, Daniel
Crawford, Willie
Crews, McKinley
Culbreath, Joshua
Davis, Gerald
Dennis, George
Ellis, Nicholson
Gordon, Bobby
Gordon, William E.
Hammie, David
Harrington, John
Harris, Cecil
Harris, Casper
Harrison, Gerald
Hart, Donald
Henley, Donald
Hollon, Herbert
Johnson, Otis
Johnson, Donald
Johnston, Raymond
Jones, Alan
Jones, Frederick
Kave, Kenneth
Keller, Verion
Keyes, William
Mathis, Harvey
McMurray, Robert
Merryweather, Ron
Mills, Charles

Morton, Linwood
Moss, Leon
Murray, Theodore
Pegram, John
Raymond, Lawrence
Rogers, James
Rogers, Benedict
Ruff, George
Sewell, John
Smith, Hosea
Smith, Henry
Solomon, Rudolph
Stansbury, Wardell
Stewart, Lebaron
Tinson, Ronald
Wade, Herman
Washington, Herbert
Waters, Edward
White, William
Wilson, Lawrence
Winder, Paul

Athletic Hall of Fame Varsity "M" Club

1971 Inductees

Inductee	Event	Year(s)
Alfred "Gator" Bell	Football-Tack	1931
Ernest "Cutie" Brown	Basketball	1930
Daniel "Pinkey" Clark	Football-Basketball	1930
	Coach	1940, 1945
Alphonso "Cottie" Cottman	Football-Track	1931
John "Stoop" Frazier	Football-Track	1931
Raymond "Tim" Hicks	Football	1930
Talmadge "Marse" Hill	Football-Basketball	1928
	Coach	1929-72
Edd "Lankey" Jones	Basketball	1930
Preston E. Lawless	Football	1928
William Cooleridge Moore	Football	1928
Arnold "Clip" Morris	Football	1930
Powell B. Sheffey	Basketball	1928
George "Hoss" Spaulding	Football-Track	1930
Russell "Speed" Sterling	Track	1932
William "Bill" Taylor	Coach	1928
Samuel "Sam" Turpin	Football-Basketball	1930
Waters "Biffo" Turpin	Football	1931
Thomas "Rap" Wheatley	Football-Basketball	1930
Robert "Bob" Williams	Football	1931
Edward N. Wilson	Historian	1916-1970

1972 Inductees

Inductee	Event	Year(s)
William "Sugar: Cain	Football-Basketball	1941
Thomas "Tank" Conrad	Football-Basketball	1934
Herbert "Hub" Crawford	Football-Basketball	1936
Carl Drake	Football-Basketball	1936
Charles "Skippy" Gibson	Football-Basketball	1934
Rufus "Legs" Hackett	Basketball	1931
Waymon Holley	Football	1941
William "Babe" Jones	Basketball	1931
William "Bill" Lampkin	Football-Basketball	1938
Ezra "Ez" Murdock	Basketball	1930
William "Mack" Payne	Basketball	1927
Wellington "Duckie" Ross	Track	1940
Maceo P. Ryan	Football-Basketball	1939
Robert "Spooks" Smith	Football-Basketball	1941
Rubin "Whirlwind" Smith	Football	1939
John "Johnnie" Sturgis	Football-Track	1935
Otis "Whataman" Troupe	Football-Track	1936
James R. Webb, Sr.	Football-Basketball	1921
James "Jim" Williams	Football-Basketball	1933
Howard "Brutus" Wilson	Football-Basketball	1934
	Coach	1957

1973 Inductees

Inductee	Event	Year(s)
Embra C. Bowie	Football-Basketball	1941
	Athletic Director	1973
Alvin "Boo" Brown	Football-Basketball	1944
	Coach	1950s
Kenneth "Ken" Brown	Football-Wrestling	1947
	Coach	1950s
Thomas "Tom" Brown	Football-Basketball	1936
John "Baby" Burdnell	Football-Track	1948
Cyril "Buns" Byron	Football-Basketball	1945
Johnathan "Unk" Campbell	Football-Track	1948
Flan "Butte" Coach	Football-Track	1950
Terry "Tippy" Day	Football-Basketball	1947
Arthur "Honeyboy" Fauntleroy	Football	1948
Clarence "Bighouse" Gaines	Football-Basketball	1945
James "Jim" Gibbs	Football-Track	1935
Joseph "Deuce" Gibson	Football-Basketball	1941
Frank "Pickle" Gordon	Football-Track	1940
Preston "Grimmie" Grimsley	Football-Basketball	1944
Herbert "Chink" Hihll	Football	1934
Jesse "Flash" Hurtt	Football-Track	1940
J. Wilbur Jordan	Football-Track	1936
Howard "Jack" Spencer	Basketball	1928
Warren "Bo" Weaver	Basketball-Tennis	1934
Gregory "G-man" Latta	Football	
Ronald "Ron" Mayo	Football	
Howard "Big Tex" Bell	Football	

1974 Inductees

Inductee	Event	Year(s)
A. Robert "Barky-Roll" Barksdale	Track	1958
Joseph "Chico" Black	Football-Track	1949
Arthur "Art" Bragg	Track	1953
Roosevelt "Rosie" Brown	Football	1953
William "Bill" Brown	Track	1951
Allen "Dickie" Burke	Basketball	1945
Charles R. Campbell	Team Physician	1930-1974
James "Stump" Carter	Athletic Founder	1916
Nicholas "Nick" Ellis	Track	1959
Samuel "Speedy" LaBeach	Track	1951
Irvin "Monk" Locust	Football	1952
Albert C. Gilbert	Football	1950
Oscar Givens	Football-Basketball	1945
Elmo "Pepper" Harris	Football-Track	1947
Ely "Tim" Howard	Football-Basketball	1951
Edward P. Hurt	Coach Athletic Director	1929-1970
Richard "Reds" Roberts	Football	1938
Charles "Bull" Robinson	Football-Track	1951
George "Choo-Choo" Rooks	Football	1951
George V. Rhoden	Track	1952
Richard "Ojay" Sowell	Football-Basketball	1938
John "Trip" Triplett	Football-Track	1952
James "Jim" Turpin	Football	1945
Robert "Bo" Tyler	Track	1951

1975 Inductees

Inductee	Event	Year(s)
William "Brownie" Brown	Swimming	1957
Earl Wesley "Early" Byrd	Football	1952
Cecil Melvin Cooper	Swimming	1955
Howard L. Cornish	Athletic Organizer	1927
Roy "Crag" Cragway	Football	1949
Joshua "Josh" Culbreath	Track	1955
Jack "The Menace" Dennis	Football	1948
Ernest "Ernie" Garrett	Basketball	1954
T. Madison "Mat" Garrison	Basketball-Track	1942
Reginald "Reggie" Holt	Swimming	1960
Williard "Toe" Jones	Football-Basketball	1947
Theodore "Ted" McIntyre	Football	1927
Carmie "Pete" Pompey	Football	1962
Lancelot L. C. Thompson	Track	1952
Robert "Bobby" Young	Football	1962
Marvin "Human Eraser" Webster	Basketball	

1976 Inductees

Inductee	Event	Year(s)
Charles "Bo" Brightful	Football	1959
William "Bill" Buford	Football	1955
Robert M. Burkett	Football	1934
Howard Lee Cornish	Basketball	1966
Bettilee "Jenks" Covert	Basketball	1955
Martin Cruise	Swimming	1956
John "Squeaks" Bubanks	Boxing	1953
Wilbur Hawkins	Football	1957
Landis "Chink" Lee	Swimming	1957
Nicholas "Nick" Lee	Track	1966
Lee Martin	Track	1962
Athelson "Thel" Nelson	Football	1949

Woodrow "Woody" Williams   Swimming   1964

1977 Inductees

Inductee	Event	Year(s)
George Robert Dennis	Track	1950
Oliver W. Dobbins	Football	1964
Clarence "Mel" Hurtt	Football	1948
Leroy Kelly	Football	1964
Donald "Pat" Patterson	Football	1955
William "Bill" Lyght	Football	1930
James "Phil" Phillips	Football	1967
James "Jimmy" Rogers	Track	1955
Lorenzo "Joints" Thomas	Football	1948
Robert "Flakie" Wade	Football	1967

1978 Inductees

Inductee	Event	Year(s)
John David Bethea	Track	1965
Kelsey Thurlow Brown	Track	1951
J. Hiram "Steepy" Butler	Football	1931
Georganna Showell Cottman	Basketball	1950
Tillman "Tex" Henderson	Football	1954
Matt "Mack" Marcus, Jr.	Football	1952
J. Laws Nickens	Football	1941
Isiah "Ted" Oliver	Football	1932
Herman "Bitsy" Wade	Track	1955
Edward "Ducky" Waters	Track	1954
Mitchell Whittingham	Football	

1979 Inductees

Inductee	Event	Year(s)
Anthony Driver Chase	Football	1929
Harry Rudolph Gross	Track & Field	1950
Laura Robinson Jones	Basketball	1938
Kenneth "Ken" Kave	Track & Field	1956
Howard Phipps Morgan	Track & Field	1954
George "Rosie" Rosedom	Football	1934
Carl "Jet" Whitted	Basketball	1953
Buck Son	Football	1959

1982 Inductees

Inductee	Event	Year(s)
Earl Banks	Coach Athletic Director	
Albert "Sonny" James	Basketball	1947
William "Ken" Freeman	Tennis	1950
Ann D. T. Koger	Tennis	1972
Willie Lanier	Football	1967
Dr. Effietee Payne	Coach	
Paul Lewis Winder	Track	1961
Roberta "Roe" Bell	Track	

1983 Inductees

Inductee	Event	Year(s)
Wilbur "Ace" Clarke	Basketball	1940
Thomas "Tex" Dean	Football	1969
Dr. Charles R. Drew	Coach Athletic Director	1926
Byron LaBeach	Track	1954
Bonnie Dayle Logan	Tennis	1972
Henry "Goose" Smith	Football	1957
Wardell Stansbury	Track	1958

Luther "Shag" Thomas   Football   1954

1985 Inductees

Inductee	Event	Year(s)
"Hubie" Brown	Track	1965
"Bobbie" Gordon	Football-Track	1958
Tom Hasty	Boxing	1952
Nathanel Hoff	Wrestling	1950
"Herb" Washington	Track	1961
Otis Johnson	Track	1955

1987 Inductees

Inductee	Event	Year(s)
J. Roland Brown	Track	1958
Walter L. Cole	Track	1961
Arnold L. Jolivet	Football	1966
Gerald B. Boyd	Football	1968
Billy Newton, Jr.	Basketball	1976
John Sykes	Football	1972

1989 Inductees

Inductee	Event	Year(s)
Robert "Bob" Berry	Track	1958
Stewart "Stu" Brooks	Coral Swimming	
McKinely "Bobby" Crevor	Track	1957
William "Tiny" Gordon	Football	1957
Russell "Russ" Jolivett	Football	1966
Robert McMurray	Track	1958
McKinley Crews	Track	1956

Sources

CIAA Bulletin, 1930, Minutes of the Nineteenth Annual Session, December 13, 1929.

James T. Taylor, Major Accomplishment of the CIAA, 1932, 21st Annual Session, CIAA.

The 20th Annual Session of the CIAA in 1931.

John O. Spencer, College Athletes, 21st Annual Session, CIAA

Chapter I: The Growing Years

CIAA Bulletin, 1930, author unknown.

Morgan's Miracle Man, William Webster Publication, unknown

Edward Hurt Offensive Football, 23rd CIAA Annual Meeting.

Chapter 2: The War Years

CIAA Bulletin, A Word About the CIAA, January 20, 1940.

Dr. Rufus E. Clement, President, Atlanta University. "The Brighter Side of College Athletics," January 20, 1940.

CIAA Bulletin, 1941.

N.C. Perrin, President, Shaw University. Speech, 28th Annual CIAA Conference.

Edward P. Hurt, Lecture on Football Offenses. 3rd Annual Florida A&M Football Clinic, June 1947.

Edward P. Hurt, "The Secret of Morgan's Defeat of Virginia State, Thanksgiving Day, 1944." *The Baltimore Afro American.*

Edward P. Hurt, "Basketball in the CIAA, 1945." CIAA Bulletin, 1946.

Chapter 3: The 1950s

John H. Burr, Address, 36th Annual CIAA Conference.

Publication, Morgan State College Public Relations Department, date unknown.

Doug Brown, *Evening Sun*, April 22, 1970

Revella L. Clay, 25th Silver Anniversary, 1953.

Talmadge Marse Hill. Ed Hurt's Retirement.

Eddie Hurt's Grizzly Bears

The guys and girls who ignored the sweat, toil, and frustration of training so that they might be able to meet their opponents in the athletic arena and emerge triumphantly as victorious "Bears."

1946 CIAA National Champions
(Morgan State University Archieves)

About the Author

Herman Wade is a retired U.S. Army Lieutenant Colonel. He attended numerous armed services schools, including the Military Assistance Institute and instructor schools while serving as an Instructor in the U.S. Army Ranger and small unit tactics committee of the infantry school. Wade served three tours of duty in South Vietnam for 24 months. He earned three bronze star medals, many commendation medals, and the Vietnamese Cross of Gallantry Medal with palm. He was the lead-off man for Coach Hurt's Flying Four Relay Team.